AN ENTERPRISE MAP OF ZAMBIA

AN ENTERPRISE MAP OF ZAMBIA

John Sutton and Gillian Langmead

IGC International Growth Centre

Published by the International Growth Centre

Published in association with the London Publishing Partnership
www.londonpublishingpartnership.co.uk

ISBN 978-1-907994-10-4 (pbk.)

A catalogue record for this book is
available from the British Library

This book has been composed in Utopia using TEX

Copy-edited and typeset by T&T Productions Ltd, London

Cover design: LSE Design Unit

Cover photographs courtesy of First Quantum Minerals and
Universal Mining and Chemical Industries Limited

Printed in the UK by Hobbs the Printers Ltd

FSC
www.fsc.org
MIX
Paper from
responsible sources
FSC® C020438

CONTENTS

ABOUT THE AUTHORS

John Sutton is the Sir John Hicks Professor of Economics at the London School of Economics.

Gillian Langmead is the managing director of Zambia-based communications firm Langmead & Baker Ltd. She is a former financial journalist and editor, and her 30-year career has involved work across Africa, Asia and Europe.

The International Growth Centre (www.theigc.org) promotes sustainable growth in developing countries by providing demand-led policy advice based on frontier research. The IGC is directed and organized from hubs at the London School of Economics and the University of Oxford and comprises country offices across the developing world. The IGC was initiated and is funded by the Department for International Development (DFID).

John Sutton's Enterprise Map Project aims to provide a standardized descriptive account of the industrial capabilities of selected countries in sub-Saharan Africa. This is the fourth volume to appear, following volumes on Ethiopia (2010), Ghana (2011) and Tanzania (2012).

ACKNOWLEDGEMENTS

The authors would like to express their appreciation to all the companies, organizations and individuals involved in the production of this book for their support, time and enthusiasm. In particular, we would like to thank the representatives of the profiled firms who agreed to be interviewed by our researchers and who provided important insights into their businesses.

The book would not have been possible without the support of the Zambian government, particularly through the acting permanent secretary at the Ministry of Commerce, Trade and Industry, Ambassador Albert Muchanga, and Miyoba Lubemba and her team at the Zambia Development Agency, who provided detailed statistical information and background research into the various sectors of the Zambian economy. The Central Statistical Office was also a valuable source of data. A number of trade associations supplied information and data, including the Zambia Association of Manufacturers, the National Construction Council and the Zambia Coffee Growers Association. Assistance in facilitating the research was provided by Felix Mwenge at the International Growth Centre. The profiles of the Chinese firms were coordinated by Qi Zhang of the London School of Economics.

Finally, the Langmead & Baker research team of Daniel Tonga, Georgina Smith, Sakabilo Kalembwe, Kenny Mvula, Margaret Samulela and Todd Jennings played a key role in the project by meeting with the fifty companies profiled.

ACRONYMS AND ABBREVIATIONS

AFIL	Agro-Fuel Investments Limited
AIM	Alternative Investment Market
CDC	Commonwealth Development Corporation
CEO	Chief Executive Officer
CNMC	China Nonferrous Metal Mining (Group) Co., Ltd
COMESA	Common Market for Eastern and Southern Africa
COMPACI	Competitive African Cotton Initiative
EU	European Union
FDI	Foreign Direct Investment
FQM	First Quantum Minerals
FRA	Food Reserve Agency
GDP	Gross Domestic Product
GTS	Good Time Steel Company Limited
HDPE	High-density polyethylene
INDECO	Industrial Development Corporation
KCM	Konkola Copper Mines Plc
KIFCO	Kabwe Industrial Fabrics Limited
LINTCO	Lint Company of Zambia
LME	London Metal Exchange
LPG	Liquefied petroleum gas
mt	Metric tonne
NCC	National Council for Construction
NCCL	Northern Coffee Corporation Limited
NCZ	Nitrogen Chemicals of Zambia
NLC	Ndola Lime Company Limited
NMC	National Milling Corporation Limited
NORSAD	Nordic/Southern African Development Community
PET	Polyethylene terephthalate
PRA	Pharmaceutical Regulatory Authority
PSPF	Public Service Pension Fund
SADC	Southern African Development Community
SAG	Semi-autogenous grinding
Stancom	Standard Commercial Corporation

TAZAMA	Tanzania Zambia Mafuta
UK	United Kingdom
US	United States
UMCIL	Universal Mining and Chemical Industries Limited
VAT	Value-added tax
ZABS	Zambia Bureau of Standards
ZAFFICO	Zambia Forest and Forestry Industries Corporation
ZAMEFA	Metal Fabricators of Zambia PLC
ZCCM	Zambia Consolidated Copper Mines
ZECCO	Zambia Engineering and Contracting Company
ZEGA	Zambia Export Growers Association
ZESCO	Zambia Electricity Supply Corporation
ZIMCO	Zambia Industrial and Mining Corporation
ZPC	Zambezi Portland Cement
ZSR	Zimbabwe Sugar Refinery

AN ENTERPRISE MAP OF ZAMBIA

Chapter 1

INTRODUCTION

Zambia's economy has grown rapidly over the past decade. Gross domestic product (GDP) per capita rose by 80% between 2000 and 2010. The copper sector played a key role in this growth, but all the other major sectors of the economy also expanded: manufacturing output grew by 50% in the same period. Much more importantly, manufacturing exports have recently surged, increasing eightfold in real terms between 1995 and 2011.

If this growth performance can be sustained for another decade, it will bring about a major advance in Zambia's economic fortunes. Can this be achieved? Any assessment of Zambia's economic prospects needs to be rooted in a detailed understanding of its industries and firms.

- What are the country's current industrial capabilities?
- Where did those capabilities come from?
- And in what areas can we reasonably anticipate a substantial advance in the country's industrial capabilities?

An Export Map

This book provides an overview of Zambian industry (agribusiness, manufacturing and construction). Within each industry, we identify the various clusters of firms ('sub-markets') and the leading firms in each cluster. We present detailed profiles of 50 firms, chosen to represent the leading firms in each cluster, thereby providing a good snapshot of Zambia's current industrial capabilities.

To place this exercise in perspective, it is helpful to begin by looking at a profile of Zambia's main export industries.[1] Three-quarters of Zambia's

[1] A similar picture might, in principle, be constructed for total production rather than just for exports, but reliable data is hard to obtain. The main message of Figure 1.1, however, would be unchanged.

export earnings in 2011 came from copper. Six firms account for (almost) all copper exports: Konkola Copper Mines, First Quantum Minerals and Operations Ltd, Lumwana Mining, Kansanshi Mining Plc, Mopani Copper Mines Plc and Luanshya Copper Mines.

The remaining quarter of Zambia's export earnings come from across a wide range of industries. However, six industries—metals, sugar, chemicals, cement, wire and cables, and flour—account for 28% of this remaining quarter. If we look at the main exporting firms, we find that a total of nine firms, along with two of the six mining companies already mentioned, together account for over half of export earnings in every one of these six industries (Figure 1.1).

Thus, 15 firms together account for over 80% of Zambia's export earnings. The dominant role played by this quite small number of leading firms puts in perspective our focus on 50 leading industrial companies: by looking in depth at this modest number of leading firms, we can obtain quite a good picture of the range of capabilities in Zambian industry, and by tracing the origin of these firms' capabilities we can learn a great deal about where Zambia's current industrial capabilities came from.

The Origin of Zambia's Current Industrial Capabilities

If we look at the origins of the 50 leading industrial companies that are profiled in later chapters,[2] we find that 24 of them started in the domestic private sector (Figure 1.2). While three-quarters of these 24 firms began as industrial companies, one-quarter were set up by companies that had long been active as trading companies. The phenomenon of 'traders becoming manufacturers' plays a key role not only in Zambia but elsewhere in sub-Saharan Africa. The reasons for the success of traders in establishing viable manufacturing concerns, to replace products they formerly imported, is discussed fully in the companion volume on Ethiopia.[3] In brief, these companies already operate a well-functioning medium-sized business, and their familiarity with the markets from which they can source inputs, and

[2] These 50 companies are listed on the contents page. Note that Zamleather is profiled separately, in Chapter 7, from its parent company Zambeef (profiled in Chapter 4) but is not counted as a separate entity when classifying the origins of these 50 companies, as illustrated in Figure 1.2.

[3] Sutton, J., and N. Kellow. 2010. *An Enterprise Map of Ethiopia*. London: International Growth Centre.

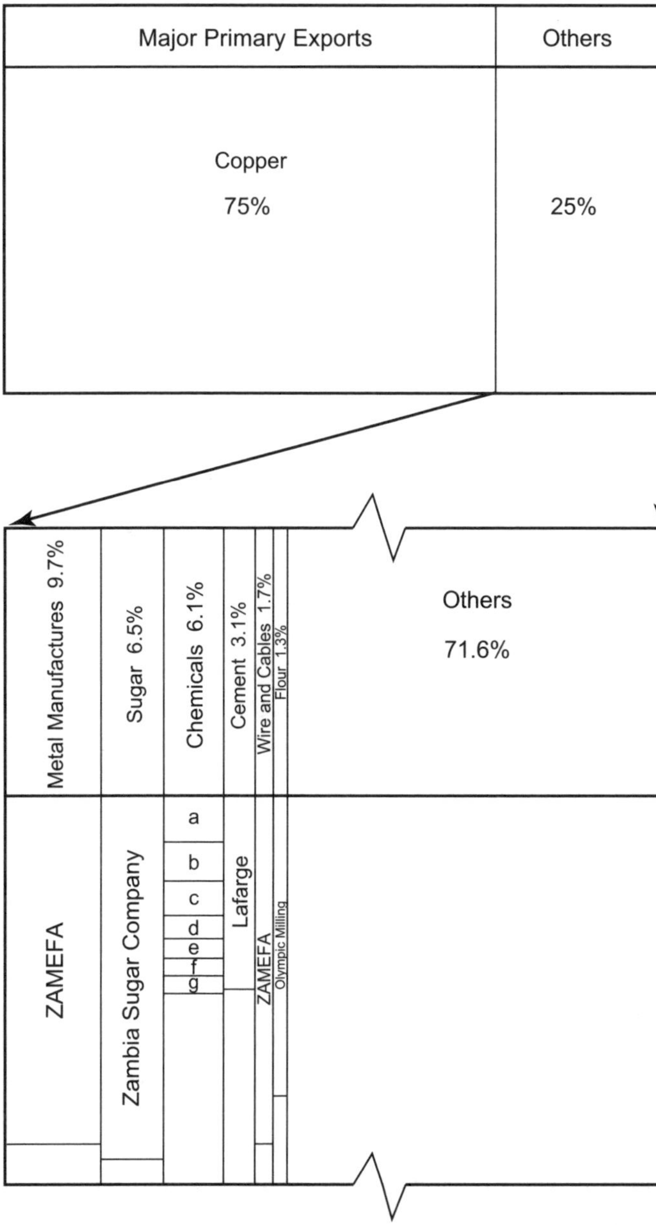

FIGURE 1.1. An export map for Zambia, 2011 ('a', Mopani Copper Mine; 'b', Chambishi Copper Mine; 'c', African Explosives Limited; 'd', Afrox Zambia Limited; 'e', Ndola Lime Company Limited; 'f', Dyno Nobel Zambia Limited; 'g', Sino-Acid Products Zambia Limited).

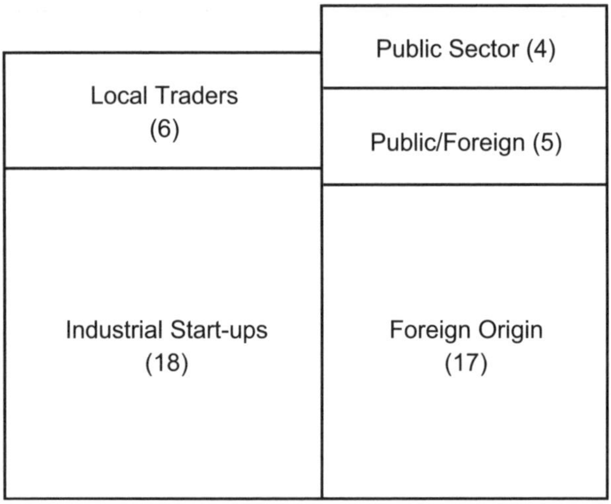

FIGURE 1.2. Origins of Zambia's leading industrial companies.

their knowledge of both potential and actual competition for the good they plan to manufacture, is deep and detailed.

A relatively high proportion of our 50 leading companies are, or originally were, foreign. If we include those that involve some form of partnership with the Zambian public sector, they account for 22 of the 50. Only 4 of the 50 leading companies began as purely domestic, public sector companies (Figure 1.2).

The Sources of Growth

Over the first decade of the new millennium, Zambia's GDP rose by a factor of 1.8 in real terms. A breakdown by sector is illustrated in Figure 1.3. Manufacturing grew by a factor of 1.5, while mining (and utilities) grew by a factor of 2.7 over the decade. The frontrunner was the construction sector, which grew by a factor of 4.0. Wholesale and retail trade grew by a factor of 1.5, while agriculture grew by a factor of 1.3.

The growth of exports is shown in Figure 1.4, and its composition is illustrated in Figure 1.5. Here, the contribution of copper is even more striking, though manufacturing exports, which rose by a factor of 8.3 in real terms between 1995 and 2011, are also encouraging. The main contributions to this increase came from metals and related products, chemicals, textile fibres and tobacco.

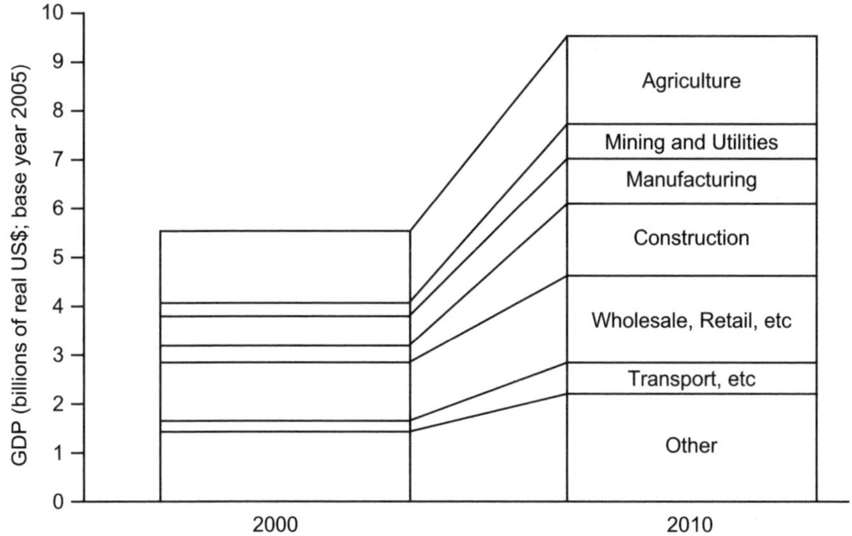

FIGURE 1.3. The change in size and composition of Zambia's GDP, 2000–2010.

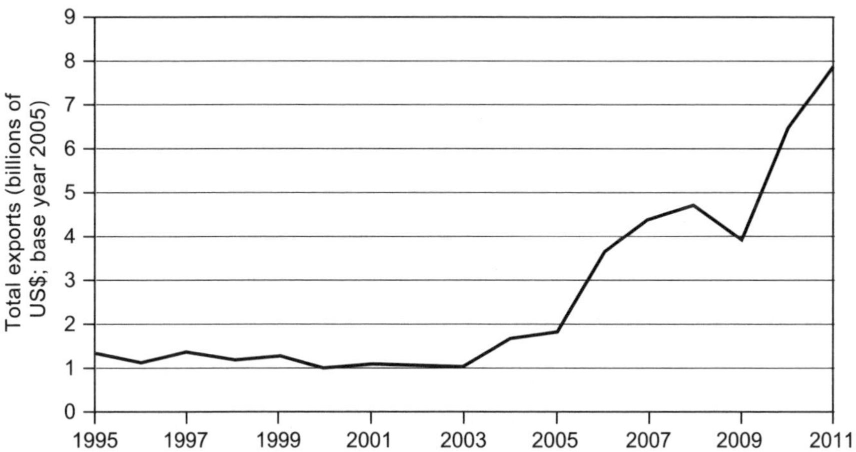

FIGURE 1.4. Total exports, 1995–2011.

This picture suggests a note of caution regarding recent discussions about Zambia's growth prospects over the coming decade. The growth in export earnings from mining in part reflects an increase in commodity prices worldwide; this is best seen as a one-off gain rather than a source of

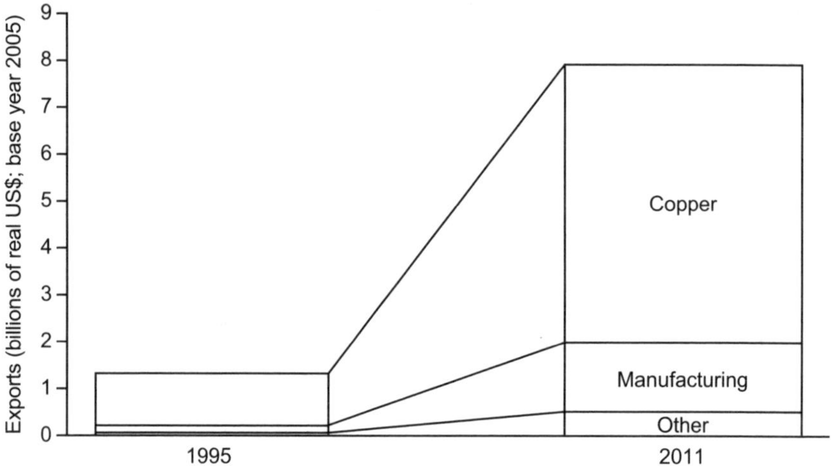

FIGURE 1.5. The changing size and composition of Zambia's exports, 1995–2011.

future growth. The contribution from construction will not last unless the economy in general continues to grow fairly rapidly, and this is unlikely to be achieved without a strong growth performance in manufacturing and agribusiness.

It is against this background that a review of Zambia's current industrial capabilities is timely: if industrial growth is to be fostered and stimulated, then it is best done on the basis of a good understanding of what the country's current industrial capabilities are and where they have come from.

Foreign Direct Investment (FDI)

We saw in Figure 1.2 that some 22 of the 50 leading companies profiled later are of foreign origin (with or without Zambian public sector involvement). This pattern is likely to be at least as pronounced in the near future if Zambia's industrial capabilities advance to a higher level, because in almost all countries that have made this advance, a high and/or rising level of FDI has been central to the process.

Between 2003 and 2011, the inflow of FDI to Zambia rose substantially, reaching 9% of GDP in 2009–11 (see Figure 1.6 and Table 1.1). Just under half (49%) of this inflow comes from two countries, Canada and Australia, who together account for 35% of Zambia's FDI stock. The UK accounted

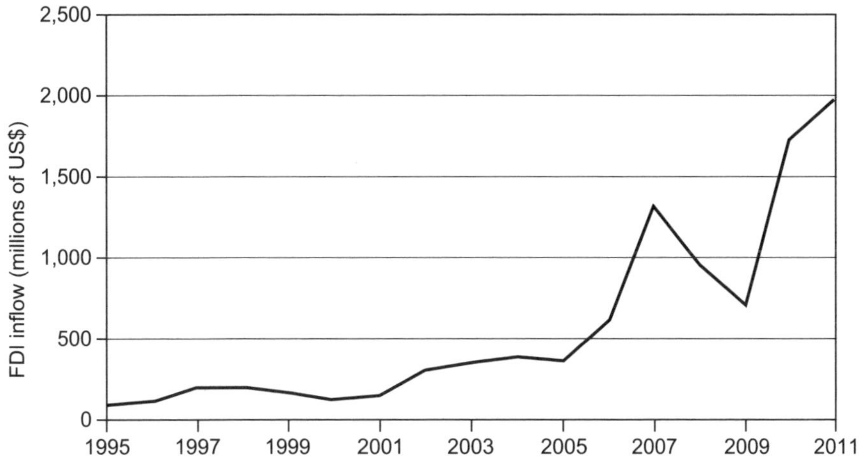

FIGURE 1.6. FDI inflow to Zambia, 1995–2011.

for 14% of the inflow and is the third largest contributor to the FDI stock, accounting for 17% of the total. China ranked ninth in terms of inflows in 2010, accounting for 2% of the total, while its contribution to the total stock was 5% (see Tables 1.2 and 1.3).

The sectoral destination of FDI is shown in Tables 1.4 and 1.5. Two-thirds of the inflow goes to the mining and quarrying sector (Table 1.4), which accounts for 66% of the stock of FDI (Table 1.5). So how much FDI goes into manufacturing? The answer is about a fifth of the total (Table 1.4). Of the total stock of FDI, only one-seventh is in manufacturing (Table 1.5). It is here that the most obvious question lies: to what extent can Zambia attract a more broadly based inflow of FDI, which will serve to broaden and deepen the country's industrial capabilities, over the next decade?

Chinese FDI

Considerable attention has recently been focused on China's role in Africa's FDI inflows. As noted above, China accounts for some 6% of the stock of FDI in Zambia. It appears to be widely believed that China's FDI activity in Africa is focused heavily on the mining sector, and furthermore that this activity is led by state-owned enterprises. Are these two beliefs justified?

TABLE 1.1. FDI flows and FDI stock for Zambia (three-year averages).

	2003–5	2006–8	2009–11
FDI flow (US$, millions)	356	959	1,469
$\frac{\text{FDI flow}}{\text{Gross fixed capital formation}}$ (%)	25.81	34.03	41.78
$\frac{\text{FDI stock}}{\text{GDP}}$ (%)	89.16	54.94	68.67
$\frac{\text{FDI flow}}{\text{GDP}}$ (%)	6.28	7.80	9.14

Source: United Nations.

TABLE 1.2. FDI inflows in 2010 by country of origin.

Country	Inflow (US$, millions)	Percentage of total net inflow
Canada	443	26%
Australia	389	23%
British Virgin Islands	271	16%
UK	250	14%
Libya	239	13%
Netherlands	78	4%
Bermuda	72	4%
France	32.9	2%
China	32.4	2%
United Arab Emirates	18	1%
Total net inflow	1,729	

The net inflow from any country may be either positive or negative. The percentage contributions of these leading countries of origin sum to more than 100% for this reason.

In order to address these issues, we examined all Chinese FDI ventures initiated in the years 2005–9, as defined by registration with the Zambian Development Authority. (As most newly registered FDI ventures take two years or so to become operational, an end date of 2009 is appropriate here.) The fraction of registered companies that become operational is modest. No reliable figure for this is available for Zambia but a useful point of comparison is that, in Ethiopia, only one-fifth of registering firms

TABLE 1.3. Average FDI stock in 2010 by country of origin.

Country	Stock (US$, millions)	Percentage of stock
Canada	1,998	18%
Australia	1,881	17%
UK	1,824	17%
British Virgin Islands	864	8%
Netherlands	775	7%
Bermuda	647	6%
China	552	5%
South Africa	551	5%
Libya	239	2%
Mauritius	218	2%
France	186	2%
Others	1,215	11%
Total	10,950	

TABLE 1.4. FDI inflows in 2010 by sector.

Sector	Inflow (US$, millions)	Percentage of total net inflow
Agriculture, forestry and fishing	13.2	0.8%
Mining and quarrying	1,141.3	66.0%
Manufacturing	373.9	21.6%
Construction	17.4	1.0%
Wholesale and retail trade	−2.2	−0.1%
Transportation and communication	179.3	10.4%
Accommodation and food	4.3	0.2%
Financial and insurance	−11.2	−0.6%
Real estate activities	−4.5	−0.3%
Other	17.8	1.0%
Total net inflow	1,729.3	

become operational. In the course of the present study, we tried to contact all 74 Chinese firms that registered in the period 2005–9. In only 17 cases (23% of the total) was it possible to confirm that the company is now operating.

The sectoral composition of the activities of these 17 firms is shown in Table 1.6. One of the 17 is not really a single firm but a cluster of

TABLE 1.5. Average FDI stock in 2009–10 by sector.

Sector	Stock (US$, millions)	Percentage of stock
Agriculture, forestry and fishing	157.4	1.6%
Mining and quarrying	6,656.8	66.0%
Manufacturing	1,518.05	15.1%
Construction	137	1.4%
Wholesale and retail trade	511.95	5.1%
Transportation and communication	567.85	5.6%
Accommodation and food	104.95	1.0%
Financial and insurance	338.9	3.4%
Real estate activities	19.85	0.2%
Other	73.4	0.7%
Total	10,086.15	

firms operating in an 'economic zone',[4] all of which are engaged in the same activity: the development of downstream activities in copper. The remaining 16 firms are widely distributed across the manufacturing sector, as Table 1.6 illustrates.[5] Moreover, the ownership of these operational firms is dominated by private enterprise; only six of them are public sector enterprises.

A Caveat

The descriptive statistics presented above, based on the 50 leading industrial companies profiled in later chapters, must be treated with caution. These 50 firms are not Zambia's largest 50 industrial companies; nor are they a random sample. Rather, they constitute a 'stratified' sample, covering

[4] The Zambia–China Economic and Trade Co-operation Zone was established following an approach from the Zambian subsidiary of the Chinese state-owned China Nonferrous Metal Mining (Group) Co., Ltd (CNMC) at Chambishi. (A second industrial park is now under construction.) The plan envisages the presence of between 50 and 60 companies; as of April 2012, 16 firms, most of them subsidiaries or affiliates of CNMC, had established a presence in the zone. These include NFC Africa Mining Plc, Chambishi Copper Smelter Limited, Sino Metals Leach Zambia Limited and Sino Acid Products Zambia Limited. Some 1,300 Chinese employees and 7,000 Zambian employees currently work in the Zambia–China Economic and Trade Co-operation Zone.

[5] This is true both of the initial pool of all companies registered and of those firms whose operational status we were able to confirm (Table 1.6).

TABLE 1.6. The sectoral distribution of FDI flows from China, 2003–9.

Sector	Registered projects	Confirmed operational
Mining[a]	13	1
Copper processing	9	3[b]
Iron and steel	7	3
Chemicals[c]	2	2
Wood and furniture	7	3
Packaging	2	2
Cotton	3	1
Vehicle assembly	3	1
Trading	2	1
Other	27	0
Total	74	17

[a] Including mineral exploration.
[b] Includes, as a single unit, the group of firms in the 'economic zone' discussed in the text.
[c] Including industrial gases.

the large majority of the country's leading industrial firms, and chosen so as to provide a fair and complete picture of Zambia's current industrial capabilities across every area of activity.

Chapter 2

WIDELY DIVERSIFIED FIRMS

A few preliminary remarks are in order.

- The fortunes of Zambian businesses have ebbed and flowed with the political and economic policies of the country, and with changes in the world copper market. Key events include independence from Britain in 1964, widespread nationalization in the late 1960s and early 1970s, and market liberalization in the early 1990s.
- The recent growth and diversification of businesses can in part be attributed to the country's robust economic growth, and in part to an underlying increase in population, from around 10 million in 2000[1] to 13 million in 2010.
- Many of the large conglomerates have evolved from small-scale family trading businesses, often started by entrepreneurs of foreign origin—mainly Indian and European—who have since become Zambian citizens.
- External sources of finance are often cited as a constraint, with most growth funded through internal cash flow.

2.1 Profiles of Major Firms

2.1.1 Trade Kings Limited

Basic details. Trade Kings was established in 1995. The firm is wholly Zambian and is located in Lusaka. It has a workforce of 1,600 full-time employees at its main branch, only 2% of which (those who come to deal with specific machinery and equipment) are non-Zambians. Trade Kings oversees a group of companies engaged in the manufacture of detergents, soaps, confectionery, soya food and other consumer products. It also has trading interests and operates a steel mill.

[1] Central Statistical Office. 2003. *2000 Census of Population and Housing.*

History. Trade Kings was started by Mohamed Iqbal Patel and close members of his family, all of Indian origin but Zambian citizens. The capital to set up the firm was raised by two family members. The firm then began to grow, and later eight other partners joined. The company is now wholly owned by 12 people, all of whom are directors of some of the firm's operations.

Having initially begun as a bakery business, the company diversified into detergent paste in 1995, before expanding into the production of toilet soap and candles in 1997/98.

Profits were reinvested to allow the company to expand into other lines of manufacturing, with sweets and confectionery added in 2001. Growth was fuelled by a government investment licence that provides tax incentives, and was motivated by the Islamic faith requirement to invest and reuse funds.

In 2005 the company expanded operations into South Africa through a subsidiary, Trade Kings South Africa, which initially imported confectionery back to Zambia but which began manufacturing in South Africa in 2009.

Current activities and products. The group manufactures and produces a wide range of consumer goods: detergent pastes, washing powder, bathing soaps, confectionery and biscuits. The company's Zambian manufacturing units are as follows.

Universal Mining and Chemical Industries Limited (UMCIL) operates a recently established steel mill in Kafue town, close to Lusaka. It is profiled in Chapter 13.

Sparlite Candle Limited produces candles for industrial and domestic use.

Royal Oak Limited produces baby cereal and custard.

Yoyo Foods Limited produces snack foods.

Swiss Bake Limited makes bread and biscuits.

Acacia Beverages produces carbonated beverages.

Organization and management. Trade Kings is managed by a board of directors comprising the 12 joint owners of the company. The board is assisted by branch managers and executives.

Supply and marketing chain. Palm oil and caustic soda are imported from South Africa, China and Southeast Asia. Fragrances are sourced from

Europe. In particular, the flavourings and colour used in the manufacturing of confectionery are sourced from the Netherlands.

Trade Kings products are distributed by the group's own trucks, although some buyers provide their own transport or outsource transport to third parties.

Much of the firm's early success, which was led by its detergent paste, was based to an important extent on the firm's access to the network of Muslim traders across the country for distribution. The traders often rely on having goods supplied on credit.

Exports. The firm exports its products to various countries in southern Africa, and in particular to those in the Southern African Development Community (SADC). It also exports to Australia, New Zealand and the United Arab Emirates.

Recent developments. The establishment of the UMCIL steel mill has also been a major milestone for the group. The firm has invested heavily in advertising, and has steadily improved its packaging and quality control.

2.1.2 Gourock Ropes & Canvas Limited

Basic details. Gourock Ropes & Canvas is a widely diversified group based in Ndola whose product range extends from ropes and canvas to plastics and packaging. Its three companies employ over 1,000 people and have an estimated turnover of US$200 million. It has a share in a palm oil refining joint venture, Gourock Industries Limited, which is profiled in Chapter 4.

History. Gourock Ropes & Canvas began as a British-owned company in the 1960s in South Africa, later expanding to Harare and Zimbabwe. The Zambian business was its third branch. It originally operated in Zambia as a supplier to mining companies, to which it sold ropes, bags and tents. The present shareholders, who are private individuals, took over the Zambian company in the early 1980s. In 1992 the company had about 40 employees, with ropes, bags and tents still being its sole lines of business.

In 1995 the company's diversification began with the setting up of a trading business to import and distribute products related to its core activities. This led the company into the import and distribution of fast-moving consumer goods.

As regional integration gained pace under the Common Market for Eastern and Southern Africa (COMESA), Gourock Ropes & Canvas established relationships with Kenyan manufacturing companies, for whom they acted as sole agents in Zambia. This led to a wider range of products being traded, including steel products (roofing sheets and steel sections).

The company undertook a substantial upgrading of its core manufacturing business (ropes and tents) in 2000, achieving ISO certification.[2]

In 2006, through Gourock Plastics & Packaging, the firm moved into the manufacture of extruded film grade plastics for plastic bags, which it had formerly imported. In 2007 it set up a new manufacturing business to produce candles. Most recently, it has set up a manufacturing facility to produce jerrycans.

Current activities and products. Gourock Ropes & Canvas continues to operate its original core business in ropes, candles, roofing sheets, tents and tarpaulins. There is also a consumer goods distribution arm, which added galvanized roofing sheets to its product range in 2006.

Gourock Plastics & Packaging makes film grade plastics for plastic bags.

Gourock Industries Limited—a joint venture partnership formed in 2007 with the Malaysian palm oil company Josofina, and Kapa Oils and Pwani Oils of Kenya—is profiled separately in Chapter 4.

Organization and management. Each division has professional managers that report to a board of directors.

Firm capabilities. Gourock Ropes & Canvas is ISO 9001:2008 certified.

Supply and marketing chain. The company imports polyvinyl chloride and canvas from South Africa, and rope and twine from Tanzania.

Roofing sheets are sourced from Kenya and India and steel coils are imported from South Africa. For its candles business, which operates as part of Gourock Ropes & Canvas and employs some 400 staff, wax is imported from China, South Africa and Singapore.

Gourock Plastics & Packaging imports granules of low-density polypropylene and high-density polypropylene from India and South Korea, and some coloured granules from South Africa.

Its packaging is sourced locally: the company buys corrugated cartons from two local suppliers. It also sources plastic polyethylene terephthalate (PET) bottles locally.

The Gourock group handles domestic distribution using its own fleet of trucks.

[2] It was the purchase of high-frequency welding machines, which allowed joins to be welded rather than stitched, that allowed the company to achieve ISO 9000 certification.

Exports. Exports constitute 10% of the total sales revenue of the group. Gourock Plastics & Packaging exports small volumes to the Democratic Republic of the Congo; Gourock Ropes & Canvas exports mainly to the Democratic Republic of the Congo and Tanzania.

Development agenda. The group would, in principle, like to outsource much of its domestic distribution. It also has some interest in moving into agro-processing and into the production of margarine and detergents.

2.1.3 Agro-Fuel Investments Limited (AFIL)

Basic details. AFIL is a transport and engineering company. Its engineering arm, AFIL Engineering Limited, has three product divisions: building supplies, office furniture and hospital equipment.

The group is also involved in cargo transportation, heavy truck spare part trading, fuel tanker hire, fuel marketing, and roads and building construction.

Group turnover for 2011 was some US$25 million. The turnover of AFIL Engineering Limited was around US$7 million for the same year. (Turnover fluctuates substantially from year to year.)

The group employs around 490 staff: 270 engineering employees under AFIL Engineering Limited, and 220 in the remainder of the group.

History. AFIL was incorporated in 1981 and began as a transport company and an operator of fuel stations, transporting fuel and agricultural commodities, having received concessions from the government for the latter.

The engineering arm of AFIL was established when the parent company acquired Lusaka Engineering Company (a parastatal that manufactured and rehabilitated trailers and made other steel products). Lusaka Engineering Company was a collaboration between Zambia and Italy, with 75% Zambian ownership. It was privatized in 1996, when 60% was sold to Amanita Zambia and was incorporated into the AFIL group.

AFIL Engineering's initial focus was on making, maintaining and repairing flatbed trailers. At first the maintenance and repair service was for the company's own fleet, but later AFIL began providing these services for other transport companies. In 2006 and 2007 it expanded into the manufacture of tipping trailers (dump trucks). In 2005/6 it began tendering for government contracts to make school desks, and from there expanded its steel furniture manufacturing operations, which now also include the production of hospital beds and office furniture.

Current activities and products. AFIL Engineering Limited has two areas of operation.

- Heavy engineering: fuel tanks, truck bodies, grain trailers, tipper trailers (dump trucks), sugarcane trailers, pontoons.
- Light engineering: steel doors and window frames, gates, school desks, office desks and chairs, hospital beds.

Organization and management. AFIL has two managing directors. One deals with the day-to-day management of the firm; the other is the company's main shareholder (a Zambian who owns 99% of the company).

Firm capabilities. AFIL manufactured 60 trailers in the first half of 2012; it has the capacity to produce nine trailers per week.

Supply and marketing chain. Special steel that meets international specifications as well as axles (two German brands) are sourced from South Africa. Truck axles are imported from France; suspension and brakes from Turkey; tyres from China; lights from South Africa; hydraulics for tipping trailers from Holland; aluminum rims from India; and school desk pipes and boards from South Africa.

The company sells locally to transporters in Zambia, to milling companies (for closed trailers to ship grain) and to farmers (e.g. trailers for crops, chicken, cattle); individuals buy a chassis and AFIL sells them a truck body.

Furniture is sold through the company's retail outlet in Lusaka.

Development agenda. AFIL is looking to the following four areas of expansion, mainly in response to demand from the mines.

- Tankers: currently this is a secondary line of business for AFIL, but it will become a primary line.
- Tippers/dump trucks: a business that has been small up to now, but which now faces increasing demand from the mines.
- Door and window frames are currently made manually to respond to a range of requests. The company plans to increase the workforce involved and to move towards mechanized production of the more popular products.
- Prefabricated structures used as warehouses and production facilities.

Challenges.

- The demand for AFIL's hospital equipment has been declining because of competition from China and India. For example, China brings in piping that is light and easy to assemble, whereas AFIL's products are much heavier. The same applies to school desks.
- Imports from South Africa are a continuing challenge. SADC tariffs were reduced quickly between 2005 and 2008, and this has allowed South Africa to dominate the regional market for trailers.
- Another challenge lies in the widespread perception among Zambian buyers that locally produced goods are inferior in quality to imported ones.

Chapter 3

FLORICULTURE AND HORTICULTURE

3.1 Sector Profile

Background and overview. Dormant until the late 1980s, floriculture and horticulture are now among Zambia's fastest growing export industries.[1] In the last two decades, liberal economic policies have encouraged entrepreneurs to set up small businesses as import and export restrictions have eased. At the same time, the government has embarked on a drive to diversify away from copper and mineral extraction to non-traditional exports, including floriculture and horticulture (Table 3.1).

Cut roses grown for export constitute 95% of floriculture output, with summer flowers accounting for the rest. Sixty different kinds of rose are cultivated and exported to Europe, either via direct sales to retailers or through auction in the Netherlands.[2] Horticultural products include fresh fruit and vegetables including asparagus, mange tout, sugar snap peas, courgettes, okra, passion fruit, mushrooms, leeks and various types of chilli.

Both industries employ large numbers of people, particularly women, in growing and packing. These employees typically support an extended family, increasing the total number of people whose livelihoods depend on earnings from these sectors. Most of the farms are situated within a radius of 60 km of Kenneth Kaunda International Airport in Lusaka, as all these enterprises started business with the intention of exporting (some now also supply small quantities to the domestic market).

Following a decline in global demand in 2009, there has been some recovery in total sales.[3] Both the floriculture and horticulture industries have made significant investments in year-round irrigation.

Supply and marketing chain. The European Union (EU) is the major market for Zambia's floricultural and horticultural products, with smaller

[1] Zambia Development Agency. 2011. *Agriculture, Livestock and Fisheries: Sector Profile* (February).

[2] Zambia Development Agency (2011).

[3] Zambia Development Agency. 2012. *Directory of Zambian Exporters 2011.*

TABLE 3.1. Floriculture and horticulture export earnings, 2005–10 (all figures in thousands of US$).

	2005	2006	2007	2008	2009	2010
Floriculture	32,094	17,839	38,248	26,910	15,411	21,950
Horticulture	20,507	23,024	37,252	36,350	11,332	11,483

Source: Exporter Audit Report 2010, Zambia Development Agency.

markets in Australia, South Africa, New Zealand and Norway. Most growers are members of the Zambia Export Growers Association (ZEGA) and vegetable producers also operate outgrower schemes. Firms need to use high-quality seeds and fertilizers and provide training and strict supervision—particularly with vegetable production—to ensure that international sanitary standards are met.

Policy context. The Zambian government has been proactive in encouraging the growth of the floriculture export industry, and it was instrumental in establishing the ZEGA as a non-profit-making association in 1984. ZEGA's key aims are to educate farmers on the safe use of agricultural chemicals, on how to work with pesticides and herbicides, and on personal and consumer safety. Great emphasis is placed on the environmental and social aspects of production of horticultural and floricultural products, in response to increased consumer concern in Europe: consumers want to know where produce has come from and whether it is ethically grown. ZEGA also promotes standards, aims to create an efficient and adequate airfreight service to encourage exports, and provides technical support and advice on sources of finance.

Challenges. Provided that labour costs remain competitive within the region, the sector should be able to expand and remain competitive in the world market. Any substantial rise in labour costs, however, could mean that Zambia would be priced out of the global market. Startup costs are high and access to the required capital can be problematic. The industry faces high costs of freight and limited bargaining power with buyers due to its relatively small export quantities; it also faces significant problems posed by currency fluctuations and unpredictable weather. As with most modern consumer-oriented businesses, there is a need for constant innovation if profit margins are to be maintained.

Competitiveness. Zambia has an ideal climate for growing flowers and has very few competitors for the cultivation of 'sweetheart roses', which constitute the country's largest floriculture export. Its main competitors in sweetheart roses are Uganda, Kenya and (increasingly) Ethiopia.

The exporting firms adhere to international standards such as the certification scheme of the British Ornamental Plant Producers organization and the internationally accredited environmental standard of the Netherlands: the Milieu Programma Sierteelt.

Export status and potential. In addition to the EU, the main export markets are the US, South Africa, New Zealand and Australia. A small but increasing volume of sales go to the Democratic Republic of the Congo.[4]

Profiles and lines of business of large firms. Zambia's leading floriculture exporter, Khal Amazi Limited, accounts for over 90% of Zambia's exports of small-headed sweetheart roses to Europe. It is profiled in the next section.

York Farm Limited is the largest producer of high-value, low-volume vegetables for export, particularly as Chalimbana, another early entrant to the market, has now closed. York Farm was set up by a European farmer and entrepreneur who had diversified into export horticulture. He then retired and negotiated a deal with the Bank of Zambia to sell York Farm to the University of Zambia in return for a share of its foreign exchange earnings. The farm was subsequently sold to a consortium of its management team and York Farm's main UK importer and distributor for less than the university had originally paid for it because profit margins had fallen.[5] The company is now once again competitive and has positioned itself in an export niche of organic produce, chiefly supplying Tesco in the UK.

Profiles and lines of business of medium-sized firms. Medium-sized businesses in the floriculture industry include Gwaza Holdings, Ambrosia Exports and Annabel Farms. These firms primarily grow for export but a very small proportion of their goods are sold on the domestic market. Esquire Roses, Enviro Flor and Kaleya Peppers are medium-sized horticultural enterprises that primarily supply the export market but occasionally sell to the domestic market if surplus produce or second-grade vegetable produce is available.

[4] Zambia Development Agency (2011).

[5] Tyler, G. 2006. Critical success factors in the African high value horticulture export industry. In *Study on Competitive Commercial Agriculture in sub-Saharan Africa (CCAA)*. World Bank.

Small-scale, informal and peripheral activities. Small-scale informal production of vegetables such as tomatoes, onions and cabbages for the local market is a significant income generator for rural and peri-urban people, with produce often collected for sale in urban markets or sold at roadside stalls.

3.2 Profile of a Major Firm

3.2.1 Khal Amazi Limited

Basic details. Khal Amazi grows and exports small-headed sweetheart roses. It recorded an annual turnover of US$18 million in 2011, with sales projected to be US$20 million in 2012. The company employs 2,170 workers on six-month contracts, seasonal contracts and longer-term contracts of over a year in duration. All output is exported to Europe.

History. Khal Amazi was established by a British enterpreneur, Greg Barnes, in 1998. He purchased Khal Amazi farm—which had two hectares of greenhouses planted with roses at the time—in the Chalimbana valley just outside Lusaka. The decision to buy the farm came about following a number of trips to Zambia during which Mr Barnes found the people friendly and the climate ideal for growing small-headed sweetheart roses. The farm was well positioned close to the airport, and sources of investment were available. The company began as a family business with capital raised from the European Investment Bank. After initial rehabilitation and further investment in five hectares of greenhouses, it became clear that production needed to increase dramatically to boost efficiency in order to make the business viable in the long run. As a result the founder sought a partner who could invest in the business; in 1999 he teamed up with PGI Group PLC, a large-scale agribusiness group in Southern Africa producing tea, cut flowers, macadamia nuts and fresh vegetables. From being a family business, the firm had now become part of a major corporation. The farm subsequently grew to 67 hectares under greenhouses across three sites: two sites of 25 hectares and a third, which is still expanding, with a current area of 17 hectares.

Current activities and products. All output consists of small-headed sweetheart roses for export. Small-headed sweetheart roses are the mainstay of the European supermarket flower market and a full range of colours is cultivated by Khal Amazi. Once harvested, the stems are graded and bunched and then stored in purpose-built cold stores. The pack houses add as much value as possible by packaging bunches in sleeves and adding flower food. Supermarket stickers are also attached.

Organization and management. The business is labour intensive, with careful supervision required 24 hours a day, 365 days a year. Staff at all three production sites, including managers, are trained locally, both in processing and packaging, and less than 1% of labour is provided by expatriate expertise. Greg Barnes is the overall managing director and the general managers of each farm report directly to him.

Firm capabilities. Zambia has a 40–50% share of the global market in small-headed sweetheart roses; the only other producers are Zimbabwe, Uganda and Ethiopia. Khal Amazi accounts for 90% of Zambia's output.

The company produces between 180 and 200 million stems per year, equating to 100 mt of airfreight per week (the company produced only 15 million stems in 1999). The partnership with PGI Group PLC gives the company access to export supply chains and supermarket contracts.

Supply and marketing chain. The main inputs are fertilizer, chemicals, packaging and freight. Most inputs and packaging materials are imported from Europe, Zimbabwe and South Africa. The company's aim is to position itself as close as possible to the consumer in the supply chain: Khal Amazi has direct contracts with European supermarkets, who audit and monitor supply and production. These supermarkets include Albert Heijn in the Netherlands, Sainsbury's, Asda and Waitrose in the UK, Aldi in Germany, and the Co-op and Bama in Sweden.

Exports. All the company's cut flowers are airfreighted to European supermarkets within three days of being harvested, using both cargo and passenger planes. The business is fully aligned with the certification schemes of the British Ornamental Plant Producers organization and the Dutch Milieu Programma Sierteelt.

Development agenda. The business is heavily labour intensive. Diversification into table grapes is an option, with expansion of up to 20 hectares in the next five years, depending on labour costs, being possible.

Chapter 4

AGRIBUSINESS AND FOOD PROCESSING

4.1 Sector Profile

Background and overview. Agriculture contributed around 20% of Zambia's GDP in 2009. This chapter considers commercial enterprises that add value to agricultural produce, but excludes floriculture and horticulture (covered in Chapter 3), beverages (discussed in Chapter 5) and cotton (covered in Chapter 6).

In what follows we look at

- animal feed,
- coffee,
- dairy,
- edible oils,
- fish,
- livestock,
- maize,
- milling
- seed,
- sugar,
- tea and
- tobacco.

Animal Feed is produced for the livestock market. The total milling capacity for animal stockfeeds is estimated at 22,000 mt per month and the market is dominated by Novatek (which is part of Zambeef Products Plc), with an estimated 30% market share, while Africa Feeds (Tiger Feeds) and National Milling each have a share of around 20%. Nutrifeeds, Simba and Olympic Milling make up the bulk of the remainder of the market.

TABLE 4.1. Export earnings by sector, 2005–10 (all figures in thousands of US$).

	2005	2006	2007	2008	2009	2010
Primary agriculture	196,975	176,913	182,702	247,638	131,693	227,223
Processed and refined foods	66,933	103,573	114,998	108,419	115,362	313,173

Source: Exporter Audit Report 2010, Zambia Development Agency.

Coffee production is undertaken by around 11 large-scale growers and 41 small-scale farmers, and it is coordinated by the Coffee Board of Zambia, with marketing activities undertaken by the Coffee Growers Association.[1]

Zambia is a high-yield producer of washed mild arabica bean coffee, including the Triple A brand. Growers are increasingly shifting to growing certified speciality coffee to gain a premium price.[2] Most Zambian coffees have historically been sold to Western Europe and Scandinavia, but a small but increasing amount goes to Japan and the US.

Zambia exported US$7.8 million worth of raw coffee in 2008, with most going to South Africa, Germany and the UK. Zambia enjoys duty-free treatment for coffee in most international markets, except in the Democratic Republic of the Congo.

Zambia has experienced a decline in the production of coffee beans in recent years. The Zambian Coffee Growers Association attributes the decline mainly to the lack of affordable long-term financing for coffee production. For viable coffee production, farmers need financing for between 8 and 13 years, and most banks are not prepared to lend on these terms.[3]

Zambia is divided into three ecological zones and coffee growers are well distributed across those zones. The crop in Zambia is dependent on irrigation and the availability of water is therefore a major factor in the choice of location. Coffee is grown at altitudes of 1,050–1,500 metres above sea level.

The Zambia Coffee Growers Association divides the coffee-growing areas into five 'coffee regions'. These are the Mazabuka/Southern, Lusaka, Kabwe/Mkushi, Copperbelt and Northern regions. Most small-scale members are located in the Lusaka, Copperbelt and Northern regions.

[1] Zambia Development Agency. 2011. *Agriculture, Livestock and Fisheries: Sector Profile* (February).

[2] Zambia Development Agency (2011).

[3] ECIAfrica Consulting (Pty) Ltd. 2012. *Potential of Non-traditional Exports in Zambia—Growth, Employment and Distribution of Wealth and Income.* London: International Growth Centre.

Plant seedlings are raised in on-farm nurseries. Two varieties of coffee are grown in Zambia: conventional varieties and semi-dwarf varieties. Coffee harvesting is done between the months of March and July.

Wet processing (primary processing) is performed at farm level by both small-scale and large-scale growers and involves machine pulping, grading, fermentation, washing, channel grading (by water) and drying.

After drying, parchment coffee is taken into a dry mill for processing. This involves hulling, grading of the resultant green beans, gravitating and bagging. For most large-scale producers the processing is done on-farm. For small-scale growers, processing is carried out at the Zambia Coffee Growers Association mill in Lusaka.

The industry is regulated by a statutory coffee board, the members of which represent government, small-scale farmers, large-scale farmers and agricultural research and extension services. The Zambia Coffee Growers Association provides coffee extension services and quality control and is responsible for all export marketing, as set out in the Coffee Act of 1989.

Dairy products include milk, butter, yoghurt, fermented milk and a small amount of cheese and cream. More than 90% of processed milk is produced by commercial farmers.

According to the Ministry of Agriculture and Livestock (formerly the Ministry of Agriculture and Co-operatives), following the privatization of the Dairy Board between 1991 and 1996, the number of processors increased from one (the Dairy Board) to more than 20. Parmalat and Finta Danish Dairies Limited have the largest processing capacity in the country, each with an installed capacity of 120,000 l per day. Output levels are, however, much lower.[4] Other major dairy firms include ZamMilk (a division of Zambeef) and Diamondale.

Parmalat Zambia is the country's largest dairy processor, in terms of output, producing fresh milk, long-life milk, yoghurt, butter and fruit juices. It employs more than 240 people. Its origins can be traced to events following the privatization of the Dairy Produce Board in 1996. Farmers in Mazabuka, Lusaka and Kitwe combined forces and negotiated with the Zambia Privatisation Agency to allow the South African milk processor

[4] Swanson reported a level of capacity utilization of 42%. (Swanson, R. 2009. Final evaluation of Land O'Lakes Zambia Title II Development Assistance Program. Report prepared for Food for Peace (USAID).)

Bonnita to buy dairy plants in these towns. Bonnita took a 70% stake in Bonnita Zambia Limited, with farmers taking the remainder.[5]

In the late 1990s, Bonnita South Africa was bought by Parmalat, the Italian dairy multinational.

Parmalat Zambia is now part of the Parmalat Africa division of the French international dairy company Lactalis, which bought a majority stake in Parmalat in 2011. Parmalat remains an independent entity with its own legal structure and stock market listing. The company has a managing director who reports to the group's head office in France.

Parmalat Zambia has an installed capacity of 120,000 l of milk per day and produces 50,000 l (40% of capacity).[6] It processes around half of the raw milk produced in Zambia by commercial and small-scale farmers (70% of which comes from the commercial farmers).

The company buys 45–50 million litres of raw milk per year, around 8% of which is from small-scale dairy farmers largely working under cooperative schemes and backed by donor funding.

Parmalat Zambia purchased most of its milk from some 21 commercial dairy farmers in 2004, and this number increased to 24 commercial farmers by 2008.

Demand for milk products continues to exceed supply, and the company reconstitutes about 200,000 l of milk per month from imported dry powder. Cheese has seen a threefold increase in demand.[7]

Dairy products are sold through large and medium supermarket chains, through smaller retail shops mostly in urban compounds and smaller towns, through Parmalat Zambia-owned metal shipping containers in urban compounds, and through informal vendors.[8]

Parmalat Zambia's exports in 2010 were between US$5 million and US$10 million.[9] In 2001 a US$5 million plant was commissioned to make long-life milk under the Bonnita brand name. The company's product range has also been extended to fruit juices and ice cream in recent years.

[5] Zambia National Farmers' Union. 16 March 2010. The ZNFU comments on the Dairy Industry Development Bill, 2010, presented to the Parliamentary Committee on Agriculture and Lands.

[6] Valeta, A. 2004. Review of the dairy industry in Zambia. Report prepared for the Regional Agricultural Trade Expansion Support Program (July).

[7] Swanson (2009).

[8] Kenny, B., and C. Mather. Undated. Milking the region? South African capital and Zambia's dairy industry. Report prepared for AfricaFiles.

[9] Zambia Development Agency. 2010. *Exporter Audit Report 2010.*

Edible oils represent an important market, dominated by Zambeef's Zamanita and Gourock Industries. However, processors complain about the import of bulk oils into the country.

Fish has traditionally been a small-scale operation in the country's natural lakes and rivers, with some commercial fish farming in fish ponds, generally supported by development projects. Lake Kariba also hosts some commercial fishing operations, largely for kapenta and bream.

Livestock is an important sector, with large-scale traditional cattle herds, particularly in Southern, Western and Central Provinces, and a number of commercial herds, particularly in Central Province. Disease has been a problem, and Zambia often faces domestic movement restrictions and is not permitted to export meat to the EU.

Chickens and pigs are also important commodities. Approximately 51 million broiler chicks are produced per year by producers ranging from small-scale to commercial farms. The sector is dominated by small-scale producers, who constitute 60% of total broiler production. Around 700,000 broilers are currently processed commercially each week, compared with 200,000 in 2009.[10]

There are eight companies with hatcheries: Hybrid Poultry Farm (Z) Ltd, Ross Breeders Zambia, Bokomo Zambia, Progressive Poultry (Tiger Chicks), Zambian Poultry Breeders, Panda Hill Hatchery, Chipata Hatcheries and Chick Masters.[11]

The Poultry Association of Zambia forecasts 15–20% per annum growth over the next five years.

Maize is Zambia's staple crop. Most maize is grown by households at subsistence level under rain-fed conditions. Large-scale commercial growers, producing under irrigation, account for around 30% of the nation's crop.

Milling. Competition in the milling sector has resulted in a focus on mechanization and production efficiency.

There are eight major flour millers. Six of these and long-established: Antelope Milling, APG Milling, Crown Royal, Mpongwe, National Milling and Olympic. Two are recent entrants: Pembe from Kenya and Africa Milling.

Zambeef (Novatek) and National Milling (Namfeeds) are the main competitors in animal feeds.

[10] Poultry Association of Zambia. 2012. The poultry industry in Zambia. Report. http://paoz.org/index.php/13-news-and-events/20-the-poultry-industry-in-zambia.

[11] Poultry Association of Zambia (2012).

Table 4.2. Zambia's sugar producers.

	Location	Hectares under sugar (estate)	Hectares under sugar (smallholder)	Production (mt)	Percentage of total national production[a]
Zambia Sugar Plc	Mazabuka	16,500	7,724	385,000	92.5
Kafue Sugar	Kafue	6,000	N/A	30,000	7.2
Kalungwishi Estates Ltd	Kasama	400	N/A	1,400	0.3
Total		22,900	7,724	416,400	100

Source: Palerm et al. (2010); Mulikelela, M., and N. Munagnya. 2010. Kafue Sugar expansion on. *Times of Zambia*, 7 July; ECIAfrica Consulting (Pty) Ltd (2012).
[a]Based on 2011 production estimates.

National Milling and Simba Milling account for around 60–70% of the mealie meal market, with the remainder shared between smaller companies.

Seed, both open-pollinated and hybrid varieties, is grown by specialized firms who conduct research and trials to develop varieties and produce breeder seeds. These firms then contract commercial farmers to grow seed for sale.

Sugar is one of Zambia's largest exports. The sugar sector is dominated by three companies: Zambia Sugar Plc, Kafue Sugar and Kalungwishi Sugar. Zambia Sugar is the largest producer, accounting for over 90% of total production (Table 4.2).

The sugar sub-sector is one of Zambia's most important export crops and accounts for 3–4% of GDP and 6% of total exports.[12] The sugar industry provides employment for around 11,000 workers, with the total number of dependents probably exceeding 75,000.[13] The sugar sector generates over US$45 million of gross export revenue annually, a figure which has almost doubled from the mid 1990s, when export earnings stood at around US$25 million.

Sugar production has risen since the sector was privatized in the 1990s, driven by FDI flows and new production technologies. Although the

[12] ECIAfrica Consulting (Pty) Ltd (2012).

[13] Palerm, J., T. Sierevogel and M. Hichaambwa. 2010. *Strategic Environmental Assessment (SEA) of the Sugar Sector in Zambia*. Report prepared for the Delegation of the European Union in Zambia.

increase in production is largely due to Zambia Sugar Plc, Kafue and Kalungwishi Sugar are growing in significance.

Both the total area planted with sugarcane and the production of sugar have been rising since 2001, apart from in the 2008 and 2009 seasons due to heavy rains in 2007. More recently, there has been a surge in output owing to major capacity expansions at Zambia Sugar Plc and Kafue Sugar.

Both the expansion plans of existing producers and proposed new investments, coupled with high world sugar prices, are expected to continue to drive growth in the industry.

Zambia is one of the lowest-cost producers of sugar in the world. It is ranked by the World Bank as the world's sixth lowest-cost producer after Brazil, Malawi, Zimbabwe, Australia and Swaziland.

Tea was until recently produced by a single producer: Kawambwa Tea in Luapula Province, a former parastatal that was sold on a competitive tender basis to Metal Distributors (UK) Limited in 1996, at which time it employed 718 staff.[14] The company was subsequently bought by Kumul Holdings of Zimbabwe in 2002, but they failed to recapitalize and the plantation has since collapsed. According to recent reports, the company is in the process of being repossessed by the government.

Tobacco contributes significantly to export earnings, accounting for around 9% of total exports. Zambia produces about 27,000 mt of tobacco a year (15,000 mt of Virginia and 12,000 mt of Burley).

There are a minimum of 500 Virginia tobacco growers in Zambia, a quarter of which are large-scale commercial farmers, with medium- and small-scale farmers generally working as outgrowers for large international tobacco buyers, who provide inputs and advice on credit.

The sizes of the crops go up to 1,000 hectares, but the majority of producers grow crops under 5 hectares or between 80 and 120 hectares.

Zambia was ranked as the ninth largest tobacco exporter in the world in 2007.

Annual exports of Virginia tobacco are valued at over US$60 million. In the last five years, exports have grown by an average of 50% per year, due in part to investment by commercial tobacco farmers relocating from Zimbabwe.

The Tobacco Association of Zambia handles storing, grading and classification, packaging and trading, and arranges outward logistics on behalf of farmers.[15] Alliance One Zambia Limited, which is profiled below, is the

[14] Zambia Development Agency. 2012. *Privatisation Status Report as at January 31, 2012.*
[15] Zambia Development Agency (2011).

largest tobacco company in Zambia, with a market share of around 41%. Africa Leaf Zambia, a subsidiary of Japan Tobacco Inc, has a market share of around 22%. Zambia Leaf Tobacco Company, a subsidiary of Universal Corporation, has a share of 19%. Tombwe Processing accounts for 13% and Associated Tobacco Company 3% of the market. The industry aims for an output of 120–150 million kg per year.

Other crops include rice, soya and wheat, paprika and other spices.

Small-scale, informal and peripheral activities. Small-scale farmers act as outgrowers to agribusiness processors and perform rudimentary processing.

Tobacco is often cured on-farm with the support of large tobacco buyers.

There are also village and town-based maize mills and abattoirs.

Supply and marketing chain. Transport logistics and the distance between growers and their markets are important issues within the agribusiness sector, particularly for those sourcing from small-scale farmers in outlying areas.

Policy context. Maize, in the form of mealie meal, is Zambia's staple food, and the market therefore receives considerable attention from government, particularly through the buying policies of the Food Reserve Agency (FRA).

The 2012 increase in minimum wages is also expected to have an impact on the sector once agricultural collective wage agreements expire at the end of 2012. Import and export restrictions on selected agricultural commodities such as maize and poultry are an area of contention, with, for example, licences required for the import of dressed chickens and for the export of maize. Maize bran, which is a byproduct of mealie meal, can only be exported during the rainy season, with an informal restriction operating during the dry season.

Challenges. A number of agribusinesses report difficulty in finding workers with the technical skills and education levels required.

Lack of transport infrastructure is a challenge, with the poor condition of roads to remoter areas and the long distances between provincial centres adding to the cost of inputs and the price of goods.

A lack of access to markets is often cited as a constraint for small-scale farmers—a problem that is again exacerbated by physical distance and the lack of reliable transport links.

Relatively high interest rates and the difficulty of accessing loans from commercial banks are also sources of concern to small and medium-sized agribusinesses.

There is 100% overcapacity in the milling sector due to an influx of new medium-sized and small entrants, and that is putting downward pressure on prices.

Export status and potential. Sugar is one of Zambia's most important non-traditional exports, along with tobacco and coffee.

Import and export bans on some crops, particularly maize, can lead to market distortions in price, and millers also complain of inconsistencies in policy elsewhere. For example, maize bran, which is a byproduct of mealie meal, can only be exported during the rainy season, with an informal restriction operating during the dry season.

4.2 Profiles of Major Firms

4.2.1 Zambeef Products Plc

Basic details. Zambeef Products is one of Zambia's most successful agro-industrial companies, with an annual turnover of US$207 million in 2011. The company is listed on the Lusaka Stock Exchange and London's Alternative Investment Market (AIM). It employs 5,500 people.

The company grows 8,000 hectares of irrigated crops and 9,000 hectares of rain-fed crops, predominantly wheat, maize and soya. It has eight beef abattoirs, one chicken abattoir and one pork abattoir; it also has 1,900 dairy cattle. The company also produces edible oils, stockfeed, bread and dairy products.

Food products are distributed through a nationwide network of Zambeef retail outlets, two wholesale outlets, seven fast-food restaurants and 20 Shoprite supermarket in-store butcheries.

The company expanded into Nigeria in 2005 and into Ghana in 2007.

History. Zambeef has its origins in 1991 when two partners—Carl Irwin, a Zambian accountant, and Francis Grogan, an Irish meat processing specialist—leased the meat-processing side of Leopard Investment Company Ltd, a small abattoir and butchery founded by Mr Irwin's father, Oliver Irwin.

The partners renegotiated existing debts and opened additional outlets but struggled with high interest rates, a lack of capital and an economic slump. The business was turned around over a four-year period by buying cattle on credit and selling for cash, while keeping overheads low.

Much of the success of the business has been due to the trust and division of labour between the two founding directors, with Mr Irwin, an accountant, overseeing finance and accounting and Mr Grogan, who has a degree in agricultural science, responsible for operations.

The business was incorporated as Zambeef in 1994. The turning point in the firm's fortunes came in 1995 when economic liberalization in Zambia coincided with a period of regional expansion in South Africa. South African supermarket chain Shoprite bought the Zambian government's privatized retail chain National Home Stores and offered Zambeef a five-year contract to supply meat to its seven outlets.

While Shoprite focused on the high end of the market, Zambeef was able to open its own retail butcher shops.

In 1996 Zambeef moved its operations to Huntley Farm in Chisamba—where its main abattoir, feedlot and cropping operations are now based—in a transaction with its cattle supplier, Zambezi Ranching and Cropping, which was looking for a long-term market for its cattle. Zambezi Ranching and Cropping acquired the farm from Lendor Agriculture and acquired a 50% shareholding in Zambeef in exchange for the farm.

In 1997 the company began growing wheat, adding chickens to its line of products in 1999, and then stockfeed, through its Novatek subsidiary.

It was listed on the Lusaka Stock Exchange in 2003 and began expansion into West Africa in 2005.

In 2008 it acquired Master Pork, an edible oils plant called Amanita (which was subsequently renamed Zamanita), a cropping business called Chiawa Farm, and a palm oil plantation. In 2011 it was listed on AIM. In the same year it bought Mpongwe Farm, giving it additional cropping capacity, and raised US$55 million through a rights issue.

The farm's total assets have grown more than threefold from US$69 million in 2007 to US$245 million in 2011.

As of 30 September 2011 the company had a market capitalization of US$107 million on the Lusaka Stock Exchange and US$54 million on AIM.

Current activities and products. Edible oils and beef each account for 23% of Zambeef's revenue, with stockfeed 11% and crops 8%. The remainder is from chicken, pork, bakery products and flour, dairy, fish, leather, West African meats and its Zamchick Inn fast-food chain.

Organization and management. The two founders act as group chief executive and director of strategy and development. The company is overseen by a professional board of directors and has recruited sector specialists to manage each division: farming, meat and dairy, manufacturing/processing, and retail.

Firm capabilities. Zambeef's size allows it to enjoy substantial economies of scale, while its vertically integrated structure enables it to control every step in the supply chain.

Zambeef slaughters around 65,000–75,000 cattle a year as well as 125,000 chickens and 60,000 pigs per year.

The Zamanita oil plant crushes soybean, producing 20% edible oil and 80% cake, which is used in chicken feed.

Supply and marketing chain. Zambeef is a primary producer of crops and livestock, but it also buys in animals from farmers across the country. Some 80% of the cattle and pigs that are processed by Zambeef are bought from small-scale farmers. It processes half of the national crop of soybean, of which 40% is grown by the company itself, with the remainder bought from farmers. It has storage facilities and modern processing equipment, an extensive trucking fleet and its own retail outlets, as well as contracts to supply the supermarket chain Shoprite.

It supplies meat to all supermarkets in the Shoprite chain and has its own chain of 122 butcher's shops, along with three wholesale outlets.

Exports. Zambeef has expanded into Nigeria and Ghana in recent years, with an abattoir and feedlot supplying Shoprite outlets there. There are also indirect exports to the Democratic Republic of the Congo through traders along Zambia's border.

Recent developments. Zambeef is upgrading and refurbishing its retail outlets and has recently invested US$8 million on upgrading its crushing machinery and adding a new solvent extraction plant for oil production.

An 800 hectare palm oil plantation is currently under development in Mpika, and new grain storage facilities are being constructed at Mpongwe.

Development agenda. Zambeef's aim is to be the most accessible and affordable quality protein provider in Southern Africa. Going forward, it aims to increase the efficiency and capacity of its primary production facilities and continue to pursue a vertically integrated business model.

It also plans to further expand its retail and wholesale distribution channels, and is planning to add a new stockfeed plant at its Mpongwe farm in 2013.

4.2.2 Alliance One Zambia Limited

Basic details. Alliance One Zambia is Zambia's largest tobacco company, buying cured tobacco from farmers, to whom it supplies finance, support and inputs. The company grades, threshes and blends the leaves before sale to cigarette manufacturers.

Turnover is around US$60 million per annum, all of which is from exported tobacco, making it one of the country's largest exporters. It employs 120 permanent staff along with 450 additional seasonal staff and 150 casual workers.

History. Alliance One Zambia is owned by Alliance One International Inc. Based in the US, Alliance One International is the entity created in 2005 from the merger of DIMON Inc and Standard Commercial Corporation (Stancom). It operates in more than 45 countries.

The US-based company DIMON was initially formed in 1995 through a merger of Dibrell Brothers Incorporated (founded in 1873) and Monk–Austin Incorporated (founded in 1907). In 1997 DIMON acquired the world's fourth-largest leaf merchant, Intabex Holdings Worldwide, S.A., making DIMON the second-largest independent leaf tobacco merchant.

Stancom, which is also US based, was founded in 1910 as a leaf tobacco merchant specializing in oriental tobacco products from the Mediterranean region. It was the third-largest independent leaf tobacco merchant in the world prior to the merger with DIMON.

In Zambia, Stancom's operations were established in 1984 as Stancom Tobacco Services Limited, initially as an affiliate of Stancom's Malawi operations, as the latter expanded into the neighbouring Eastern Province of Zambia.

After the global merger of Stancom and DIMON, the new company registered Alliance One Zambia Limited in 2007, while its precursor Stancom Tobacco Services is now dormant.

Current activities and products. Alliance One Zambia works with around 8,000–10,000 farmers: commercial tobacco farmers, smallholders and grower associations throughout Zambia. It buys 10–11 million kg of flue-cured tobacco, 6–10 million kg of Burley tobacco and 600,000–1 million kg of dark fired tobacco.

Organization and management. The company is run by a managing director and a team of specialists that includes agronomists.

Supply and marketing chain. Finance, technical support and inputs such as seeds, fertilizer and chemicals are provided to farmers on credit.

Some 32 commercial farmers account for around 60% of purchased crops, small-scale farmers account for 30%, and the remaining 10% is provided by medium-sized farmers, which represent the fastest-growing sector of supply and an area where yields can be improved; the constraining factor is the availability of skilled labour.

The tobacco is cured by the farmer, with support from Alliance One Zambia in terms of credit and design for barns. The company buys most of its tobacco at its 12 markets around the country, with the remaining 30% being bought through the Tobacco Association of Zambia.

Burley tobacco, grown mainly in Eastern Province, is processed at the company's factory in Lilongwe, Malawi, along with fire-cured tobacco, while flue-cured tobacco is sent to Zimbabwe for processing.

Transport is contracted out by annual tender, both for internal transport and for export. Regional tenders are held for input supply.

One important issue in the market is 'side-buying', under which middlemen buy crops from farmers, usually for cash, that have previously been pledged under outgrower contracts to large companies that have provided the farmer with fertilizer, seed and pesticides on credit terms, making it harder to recover the credit extended. Alliance One Zambia would like to see a tighter enforcement of the Tobacco Act and credit control regulations, helping to make the nation's crop compliant with international standards on issues such as child labour and reforestation. Alliance One Zambia is already compliant with these requirements.

The economic and political turmoil in Zimbabwe has resulted in an exodus of commercial tobacco farmers from that country. It has also provided additional market opportunities for Zambian tobacco as some former Zimbabwean farmers have set up operations in Zambia and buyers have focussed more attention on buying from Zambia rather than Zimbabwe. The drop in supply from Zimbabwe has also prompted growth in supply from Brazil, however, which has added competition.

Exports. All of Alliance One Zambia's tobacco is exported, having been presold to the main cigarette manufacturers such as Philip Morris International, British American Tobacco, Imperial Tobacco and Japan Tobacco International. It is often shipped directly to these buyers' factories in China. The Zambian office makes direct contracts with buyers and the tobacco is shipped with traceable labels identifying it as originating in Zambia.

Zambia's tobacco is considered to be of good quality, but the total volume of output is low, constituting less than 1% of global output.

Recent developments. The company is planning to build a US$45 million 500,000 square metre plant in Lusaka in the government's new Multi-Facility Economic Zone. It is expected to be the largest tobacco processing plant in Africa, with an initial capacity of 30,000 mt.

Development agenda. The company has continued to expand crop production to meet demand for its planned new factory in Lusaka. It has been working with small-scale farmers to encourage them to diversify their income by growing other crops such as wheat, seed maize and soya, as well as encouraging reforestation.

4.2.3 Zambia Seed Company Limited (Zamseed)

Basic details. Zamseed pioneered the production of certified seed in Zambia. It was incorporated in 1974 but commenced active business in 1981. It was initially a semi-parastatal company that was responsible for the production and marketing of all types of seed with the exception of cotton and tobacco.

History. Zamseed was formed as a partnership between the government of Zambia, the Swedish government and local seed growers in order to develop seed research. Technical assistance was provided by the Swedish plant breeder Svalöf Weibull AB and financial support was provided by the Swedish government's venture capital fund for emerging markets (Swedfund).

In 1999 the government reduced its shareholding from 40% to 37.5% under the state privatization programme, and the combined shareholding of the Zambia Co-operative Federation and the Zambia Seed Producers Association was reduced from 40% to 10%. As a result of this, Svalöf Weibull's shareholding increased from 10% to 27.5% while Swedfund International AB's shareholding increased from 10% to 25%.

The company is now privately owned and run by its staff, with the company's management holding a majority share. The company's current turnover is about US$10 million per annum. The company employs 77 permanent staff and about 200 seasonal ones. After liberalization of the economy in 1991/92, seed companies from South Africa and Zimbabwe entered the market. Zamseed faced challenges in its distribution network, and these problems were exacerbated by the collapse of institutions such as Lima Bank and the Zambia Co-operative Federation, which supported agribusiness.

The company had been selling material that was developed and produced by the government's Mount Makulu Research Station in Chilanga (about 20 km south of Lusaka), but the supporting distribution network collapsed, leading to difficulties in producing even small amounts of seed.

Current activities and products. Zamseed produces various types of certified seeds for both the local and export markets. The product range includes certified varieties of maize, soybeans, millet, groundnuts, sorghum, cowpeas, sunflowers, wheat, beans and vegetables. Due to market demand, Zamseed has also gone into vegetatively propagated planting materials, including sweet potato vines and cassava cuttings.

Maize. Maize seed is the company's main product and it accounts for 70–80% of sales. Planting of maize seed varieties depends on the rainfall pattern or the agro-ecological location of the grower. Low-rainfall areas are planted with early maturing varieties; medium-rainfall areas use medium maturing varieties; high-rainfall areas use long season varieties.

Soya beans. Kaleya and Magoye are the two available varieties. Both take an average of 115–130 days to mature and have a yield potential of 3.0 mt per hectare.

Pearl millet. Two varieties are available: Lubasi and Tuso. These take between 125 and 130 days to mature with average yields ranging between 1.5 mt to 2.0 mt per hectare.

Groundnuts. Zamseed has three varieties: Chipego, a 110-day crop with a potential yield of 1.5 mt per hectare; MGV-4, a 130-day crop with a potential yield of 2.5 mt per hectare; and Chalimbana, a 145-day crop with a potential yield of 1.2 mt per hectare.

Sorghum. Two varieties are available: Kuyuma and Sima. Kuyuma is a 105-day variety with a yield of 5 mt per hectare, while Sima is a 120-day variety with a yield of 7 mt per hectare.

Cowpeas. Lutembwe and Bubebe are the two varieties on offer. The yield potential of both is around 1.5 mt per hectare.

Sunflowers. Currently the company has two varieties: Milika and Record. These are of 100–125 days maturity with average yields of 1.5–2.0 mt per hectare.

Wheat. Four varieties are available. All are winter varieties averaging 115–125 days to mature and with yields varying from 8.0 to 9.0 mt per hectare. The varieties are suitable for most of the southern regions of Africa.

Beans. Lyambai and Chambeshi are on offer to the market. These are 120-day varieties with average yields of 2–3 mt per hectare.

Vegetable seeds. Zamseed has a wide range of available vegetable seeds including both hybrids and open-pollinated varieties. Indigenous vegetable seeds of high nutrition and value are also produced.

Organization and management. The board of directors includes both major shareholders and representatives of management. The research and production director runs the Zamseed farm. The management team includes a finance manager, a marketing manager and regional sales mangers.

Firm capabilities. Zamseed has the capacity to produce up to 17,000 mt of seed per annum.

The company currently produces about 4,000 mt of maize seed per annum (as opposed to the 10,000 mt per annum it produced when it was a semi-parastatal company). Its total seed output, including soybeans, amounts to 6,000 mt per annum.

Zamseed now accounts for about 25% of the domestic market for seeds, as opposed to the 100% market share it had in the 1980s.

Competition. When the Zambian economy was liberalized, new players came onto the seed market. Among the first were Seedco International Zambia Ltd, Pannar Seed (Zambia) Ltd, MRI Seed Zambia Ltd, Pioneer DuPont Zambia Limited and Monsanto. Competition introduced different challenges: in particular, seed-borne diseases that affected Zamseed's materials.

Genetically modified seeds are currently banned in Zambia.

Supply and marketing chain. Zamseed has five main depots for distributing its products in Kitwe, Chipata, Mazabuka, Chisamba and Kapiri, with a total holding capacity of 1,000 mt. The seed is transported from Lusaka and kept in these depots for easy distribution to other parts of the country. The depot managers are responsible for market intelligence in their areas.

In places where the company does not have depots, it engages a network of well-established agents with warehouses, transport and other facilities to sell and distribute its products.

The company also works with agro-dealers and stockists.

Exports. The main export markets are the Democratic Republic of the Congo, Tanzania and Zimbabwe. Smaller volumes go to Angola, Egypt, Kenya, Eritrea, Madagascar, Malawi and South Africa.

Recent developments. The company has realized that it needs to supply legume seeds to farmers, which are important for crop rotation and retention of nitrogen in the soil.

The company recently introduced upland rice to its range of products.

Development agenda. The shift from a parastatal to a private company has enabled Zamseed to be more flexible and strategic. The company is currently seeking partners who will improve its efficiency through the acquisition of new technologies. The company predicts an increase in exports and aims to expand into Tanzania and elsewhere in East Africa.

4.2.4 National Milling Corporation Limited (NMC)

Basic details. NMC is Zambia's largest miller of cereals. Turnover is about US$75–80 million per annum and the company has 550 permanent employees and between 200 and 400 additional workers at peak times.

History. The company began as Shapiro's Milling Company, started by an immigrant from Palestine who came to what was then Northern Rhodesia in the early 1920s. The company was nationalized as the National Milling Company in the late 1960s, after independence, and became part of the Industrial Development Corporation (INDECO), which in 1971 was amalgamated into the government's parastatal investment arm Zambia Industrial and Mining Corporation (ZIMCO).

Under the liberalization of the late 1990s the company was privatized in 1996 with ZIMCO selling its 51% share to Erabus BV, a Dutch subsidiary of Anglo American of South Africa, which previously owned 24.5% under preemption rights, and Namib Mills, which was brought in to manage the company after the third shareholder, Dalgety Spillers of the UK, opted not to exercise the preemption rights on its 24.5% holding. The company was technically insolvent at the time of the privatization, however, and in 1998 it was sold to the US-based company Seaboard Corporation, who renamed it the National Milling Corporation.

Current activities and products. The company processes maize, wheat and soya, and polishes local rice. It trades in imported rice, salt, sugar and cooking oil. It is also the second largest producer of animal feeds by volume, which it sells under its Namfeeds brand.

The company claims a 25% share of the flour market, a 30% share of the mealie meal market, and a 40% share of the stockfeed market.

Organization and management. The company has a board overseen by a chairman in the US and a company secretary in Zambia. It has a local managing director who oversees five departments, with seven managers reporting directly to him.

Firm capabilities. The company is operating at 90% of its rated capacity on animals feeds and at 70% of capacity for mealie meal and flour. It has capacity to mill 60,000 mt of wheat and 130,000 mt of maize per annum.

NMC has two manufacturing sites in Lusaka and one in Livingstone, a distribution branch in Kitwe, and 45 sales outlets.

Supply and marketing chain. Some 85% of raw materials are bought locally, with white rice imported from Thailand, Vietnam, India and Pakistan. Micronutrients for stockfeed are imported from South Africa and India.

Soy beans and wheat are bought from commercial farmers. Most maize comes from small-scale farmers, who produce a better-quality crop than commercial farmers. Half of the company's maize is bought via the FRA, with the remainder being bought at the company's factory gates in Lusaka and Livingstone or through small traders.

The company buys 50,000 mt of wheat a year for flour. It buys 100,000 mt of maize a year, 75% of which is used for mealie meal and 25% for stockfeed; 25,000 mt of soybean, all of which is used for animal feed; and 2,500 mt of paddy rice.

Cooking oil is a byproduct of the company's soybean-processing activities. The crude oil is refined by third parties and then returned to NMC to be sold under its Mother's Pride brand.

NMC sells to all main retail chain outlets in the country. Only 2% of flour is sold in retail packs, with the remainder sold in bulk to bakeries and wholesale customers.

Some 35% of the company's transport needs are fulfilled by its own fleet of 28 trucks.

Exports. Exports are made mainly to the Democratic Republic of the Congo, with smaller amounts to Mozambique and Malawi.

Recent developments. Increased competition has caused NMC to improve mechanization and efficiency, and it is upgrading and refurbishing machinery as well as adding silos.

Development agenda. A bakery is under construction, and the company is considering upstream integration into farming.

4.2.5 Hybrid Poultry Farm (Zambia) Limited

Basic details. Hybrid Poultry Farm (Zambia) is the largest poultry producer in Zambia. Its turnover is US$35 million per year and it has around 1,100 employees.

History. Hybrid Poultry Farm (Zambia) began as a family business when it was incorporated as Hybrid Poultry Farm (Northern Rhodesia) Ltd in 1961. It subsequently became Hybrid Poultry Farm (Zambia) Limited upon independence. It was then bought by Booker Tate Ltd, which sold it in 1998 to a management buyout backed by the Commonwealth Development Corporation (CDC). CDC and the previous owners sold the business in 2003 to Hybrid's current owners, a Kenyan family consortium, who took full control in 2004.

Current activities and products. The company produces day-old chicks for sale and processes broiler chickens through its subsidiary company Verino Agro Industries.

Organization and management. The managing director of Hybrid Poultry Farm (Zambia) also oversees Verino Agro Industries, as well as sitting on a local board along with a finance director and chairman. He oversees general managers and regional department heads for processing, production, sales and operations.

Firm capabilities. The company has seven broiler breeding farms and two commercial hatcheries in Lusaka and the Copperbelt. It produces approximately 50% of the country's broiler day-old chicks and pullet requirements. It has been chosen by its supplier, Cobb Vantress, as the best breeder of grandparent stock in Europe, Africa and the Middle East.

Some 25% of its day-old chicks are reared in-house and through contract outgrowers. Slaughtering and dressing are done by its subsidiary Verino Agro Industries, and the dressed chickens—mostly frozen—are sold under the Country Choice brand name.

Following a recent increase in its capacity, the company is now running at about 60% of capacity. Demand has been growing at 15% a year for the last eight years, reflecting national increases in disposable income, a rise in beef prices and improved standards and breeding performance in the industry.

Supply and marketing chain. Hybrid imports broiler grandparent chicks from Cobb Vantress in the UK. Hybrid then breeds the parents at three farms in the Copperbelt and six around Lusaka. The subsequent-generation day-old chicks, produced by the company or through contract outgrowers, are sold to commercial and small-scale farmers. Grandparents are reared at the company's 2,000 hectare farm near Kabwe. Biosecurity is of prime importance at all sites.

The company sources maize from commercial and small-scale farmers and from feed companies.

Some 75% of broiler chicks are sold to customers as day-old chicks, with the majority going to small-scale farmers, of which the company has 10,000 individual customers in the Copperbelt alone. Chicken production is considered a strong cash flow activity with low start-up costs, which makes it appropriate for small farmers.

Hybrid distributes chicks countrywide using its own vehicles, mostly to agents who sell through their own outlets. The company has a policy of focusing on its core business and has chosen not to diversify into the supply of stockfeed.

Some 25% of the company's broiler chicks are reared on its own farms and then slaughtered and dressed at its abattoir in Chongwe by its wholly owned subsidiary Verino Agro Industries Ltd. They are sold under the Country Choice brand, mostly as frozen chickens, directly to supermarkets and fast-food outlets. Verino is one of only three plants in the country that has HACCP ('Hazard Analysis and Critical Control Points') and ISO 22000 certification. It is also regularly audited by the Kentucky Fried Chicken company, and it is halal certified.

Verino also processes chickens under contract for Eureka Chickens.

In addition to broilers, layer parents are bought from Isa in France, fertilized eggs are produced, and the resultant day-old pullets are sold to both commercial and small-scale table egg producers.

Exports. Hybrid sells mainly on the domestic market but has a small export business to neighbouring countries, exporting fertilized hatching eggs to its sister companies in Kenya and Tanzania. Layer chicks and frozen chickens are exported indirectly to the Democratic Republic of the Congo. Exports account for 1–2% of sales.

Recent developments. In recent years the company's breeder farms and hatcheries have been upgraded and expanded and it maintains a rolling programme of capacity expansion. A US$3 million refit of its processing plant has also recently been completed.

4.2.6 *Zambia Sugar Plc*

Basic details. Zambia Sugar processes sugarcane grown on its own estate and by outgrower farmers, and is Zambia's largest single non-traditional exporter.[16] The company's turnover for 2012 was US$285 million. Its production volume was 374,000 mt, of which 238,000 mt was exported.

The company is listed on the Lusaka Stock Exchange and at peak it employs close to 6,000 people, 2,000 of whom are permanent staff.

History. Zambia Sugar began operations in 1960 as the Ndola Sugar Company Limited, with a sugar estate on the Zimbabwe border at Chirundu and a sugar refinery in Ndola founded by UK company Tate & Lyle. In 1963 Tate & Lyle began trials at Mazabuka and a year later, at independence, Ndola Sugar's name was changed to Zambia Sugar Company Ltd. The company began developing the Mazabuka estate in 1966. The estate and factory were completed in 1968 at Nakambala, Mazabuka, with a design capacity of 80 mt crush per hour.

In 1972 state-owned investment vehicle INDECO acquired a 51% stake in Zambia Sugar under the government's nationalization programme, increasing that stake to 78% in 1975, with Tate & Lyle retaining 10.8%.

In 1976/77 the factory at Nakambala was expanded, and by 1982 an outgrower scheme was set up with the help of the CDC and additional funding from Barclays Bank and the Development Bank of Zambia. In 1983/84 the capacity of Zambia Sugar's Nakambala mill was expanded to 150,000 mt per annum, and by 1992 the company had 12,000 hectares of cane under cultivation.

The company was floated on the Lusaka Stock Exchange in 1995 and renamed Zambia Sugar Plc, at which point Tate & Lyle acquired 40% and CDC 31% under the government's privatization programme. Tate & Lyle later took its stake up to 50.9% with the government retaining 18.1%. The company was listed on the Lusaka Stock Exchange in 1996.

In 2001 Illovo Sugar Limited, which is 51% owned by Associated British Foods, bought Tate & Lyle's sugar business, and under a mandatory offer to minority shareholders increased its stake in Zambia Sugar to 89.71%. In 2009 the company bought Nanga Farms and undertook major expansion funded by a rights issue that decreased Illovo's share to 81.55%.

[16] Non-traditional exports are defined as all exports other than copper and cobalt.

Current activities and products. Zambia Sugar's operations and mill are based at its Nakambala Estate in Mazabuka, where it crushes sugarcane to extract raw sugar, around a tenth of which is then refined. Syrup, caster sugar and speciality sugars are also produced in small quantities. Sugar for domestic consumption is required by law to be fortified with Vitamin A.

Organization and management. Zambia Sugar's managing director also acts as managing director of the firm's operations in Malawi and Tanzania. He reports to the operations director of Illovo Sugar.

There are local managers for agriculture, factory operations, finance, human resources, risk management, marketing and corporate affairs, all of whom are supported by Illovo in South Africa. Specialists from Associated British Foods provide input on safety and quality assurance.

Firm capabilities. The company has the capacity to produce 400,000 mt of raw sugar per annum.

Supply and marketing chain. Zambia Sugar grows sugarcane on around 17,000 hectares of its own land in Mazabuka and works with 16 groups of commercial and small-scale farmers that grow on a further 10,000 hectares between them. Cane is transported to the factory by two contractors and by the company's own vehicles. The company generates all of its own power needs from a 40 MW bagasse-fired power plant.

Most of Zambia Sugar's refined sugar is sold in bulk to industrial users such as beverage manufacturers and manufacturers of biscuits and sweets. These buyers take around 20,000 mt between them.

Some 150,000 mt is sold domestically as household sugar and brown sugar. The latter is unrefined but has a particularly light natural colour.

Zambia Sugar has a domestic market share of around 90–95%. The other producers are Kafue Sugar, producing between 20,000 and 30,000 mt per annum, and Kalungwishi Sugar (which produces under the brand Kasama Sugar), with an output of less than 5,000 mt per annum.

Molasses are sold as animal feed both to the local market and to South Africa.

Exports. Zambia and Malawi are considered to be among the best places in the world to grow sugarcane in terms of quality and yield, but Zambia produces less than 1% of global output.

Some 100,000 mt of sugar is exported to the Democratic Republic of the Congo, Rwanda, Burundi, Zimbabwe and other neighbouring countries. Over 120,000 mt per annum is exported to the EU as raw sugar for refining.

Preferential pricing for Zambian sugar in the EU is now being phased out, so Zambia Sugar needs to become more competitive on world markets. It still has long-term contracts with European refineries at slightly higher than world market prices.

Regional markets such as the Democratic Republic of the Congo are seen as the most promising markets for growth.

Recent developments. In 2009 Zambia Sugar undertook a major expansion programme, spending US$200 million to increase capacity from 230,000 mt per annum to 440,000 mt per annum.

More recently, the company has been exploring new ways to add value, by selling Fair Trade sugar and speciality sugars to Europe.

Development agenda. A feasibility study is currently under way on installing an ethanol plant.

4.2.7 Gourock Industries Limited

Basic details. Gourock Industries is based in Ndola, where it refines crude oil into edible oils, soaps, fats and powders. It employs over 500 people and has an estimated turnover of US$100 million per annum.

History. Gourock Industries is a joint venture partnership formed in 2007 between Gourock Ropes & Canvas Ltd, Malaysian palm oil company Josovina Commodies Sdn Bhd, Kapa Oil Refineries Ltd and Pwani Oils Ltd of Kenya, and other shareholders.

Current activities and products. Gourock Industries produces edible oils, soaps and fats through the fractionation of crude palm oil imported from Indonesia and Malaysia.

Organization and management. Gourock Industries is headed by a chief executive officer (CEO) who is a specialist in food technology. He has a team of qualified managers and reports to a board of directors.

Firm capabilities. Gourock Industries is currently operating at 60% capacity in its refinery, with half of its production sold domestically and half exported, mostly to the Democratic Republic of the Congo and Malawi. It has a refinery capacity of 500 mt per day, a capacity of 100 mt per day in the soap plant and a capacity of 2 mt per day in the fat plant.

Supply and marketing chain. Gourock Industries has an estimated 45% share of the Zambian edible oils market and began exporting to Malawi and the Democratic Republic of the Congo in 2011.

It buys crude palm oil from Indonesia and soya from Argentina, but it hopes to buy 30–40% of its soya from the local market once its crushing plant comes on stream.

Granules are sourced from South Africa and the Far East and made into high-density polyethylene (HDPE) plastic containers for the company's products.

The company sells directly to large retailers and wholesalers through its own sales force.

Gourock Industries distributes domestically using its own fleet of trucks.

Exports. Gourock Industries exports around US$50 million worth of products a year, mainly to the Democratic Republic of the Congo and Malawi, and the company is currently exploring export possibilities in Zimbabwe and Angola.

Recent developments. Gourock Industries is now focusing on backward integration of edible oils, working towards a seed crushing unit. Its intention is to achieve full integration of its farming operations: from farm and seed crushing through crude oil, and on into distribution to customers.

Development agenda. In principle, Gourock Industries would like to outsource much of its domestic distribution. It also has some interest in moving into agro-processing and into the production of margarine and detergents.

Gourock Industries is planning to acquire a multi-seed crushing plant, which will take its oil refinery up to full capacity. The company also has plans to expand into farming of soybeans.

4.2.8 Speciality Foods (Z) Limited

Basic details. Speciality Foods (Z) manufactures a wide range of food products at its base in Kitwe. Its turnover is approximately US$3.6 million per annum and it has 150 full-time employees.

History. The company was incorporated in 1966 as one of two Zambian subsidiaries of Denton and Kennedy, a Zimbabwean holding company. In 1983 Speciality Foods (Z) was taken over by Chibote Limited, a Zambian holding company, through a worldwide acquisition of J. L. Morrison.

A fire destroyed 60% of the firm's factory in 1986, and Chibote then sold the company to a Zambian national, Chad Kaunda, who had previously worked with Chibote's owners.

Current activities and products. Speciality Foods (Z) makes more than 50 food products in six categories: sweets, snacks, peanut products, baby foods, powders and liquids at its factory in Kitwe. The company manufactures to order for large retail shops including Shoprite, Pick n Pay and Spar, and supplies over 100 wholesalers spread across the country.

Organization and management. The chief operations officer, Chibwe Kaunda, is the son of the founder, and he reports to a board consisting of family members. Senior managers are recruited from outside the family on the basis of professional qualifications.

Firm capabilities. The company manufactures to high hygiene standards and products are tested in the company's laboratory at every stage of production from incoming raw materials through production and finished goods to ensure conformity in terms of quality and specification. Products are also tested in University of Zambia laboratories and by the Zambia Bureau of Standards (ZABS).

In 2011 the company produced about 300,000 cases (of ten units per case) of various products. Production capacity is about 500,000 cases of various products per annum.

Supply and marketing chain. Specialty Foods specializes in the production of food that adds value to locally sourced agricultural produce. Its products include groundnuts (for peanut butter), soybeans (for soya flour), maize grit (for maize-based corn snacks), packaged honey and sugar (for icing sugar and caster sugar).

It is the country's single largest buyer of groundnuts and honey produced by small-scale farmers.

Speciality Foods (Z) produces from the Copperbelt and supplies all markets on a daily basis. It produces only to order so as to minimize inventory costs.

It also packages products in small packs that are targeted at low-income communities, in order to widen its market.

Challenges. Problems with access to cheap finance, competition from imports and, more recently, new minimum wage legislation are among the key challenges the company faces.

Exports. Speciality Foods (Z) exports small amounts to the Democratic Republic of the Congo through traders who come to Zambia.

Recent developments. In 2008 the company invested in new machinery that increased production capacity, reduced unit costs and improved packaging and health standards.

Development agenda. The entry to the Zambian market of large retailers such as Pick n Pay and increased orders from existing retailers such as Shoprite give Speciality Foods (Z) a rising level of demand and it plans to increase production capacity to meet this. The company has considered three strategic developmental options: sell the company to a bigger company, merge with another company, or float shares on the Lusaka Stock Exchange. However, management wants the firm to remain in the hands of the family, and no decision has yet been made.

The company is considering seeking further funding to increase its working capital to finance its various raw materials requirements, especially for the large seasonal commodities such as groundnuts, soybeans, honey and sugar.

4.2.9 Northern Coffee Corporation Limited (NCCL)

Basic details. NCCL is Zambia's largest coffee estate and has 124 permanent employees. Its annual turnover is US$2.5 million.

History. Zambia Coffee Company was established in 1985 as a parastatal owned by the Zambian government. In 1997 it was privatized and became the African Plantation Company. In 2001 it changed its name to Kasama Coffee Corporation. In 2010 the company was under receivership and there was no production.

In 2011 the company became Northern Coffee Corporation Limited; it is 49% owned by Zanaco Bank, 43% by Standard Chartered Bank and 8% by the Zambia Development Agency. At this time the company restarted operations with initial capital of US$1.2 million.

In September 2012 global agribusiness company Olam International Limited bought the company for US$6.15 million through a bidding process organized by the Zambia Development Agency.

Current activities and products. The firm grows wheat and soybeans, planting these two seasonal crops in between the longer-term coffee bushes.

The company is currently cultivating 1,245,000 coffee seedlings in a nursery, which is enough to plant out 350 hectares.

Organization and management. The company is managed by Olam International Limited.

Firm capabilities. NCCL's assets consist of five estates on 5,866 hectares of land in Northern Province. Approximately 1,580 hectares across three of these estates were previously cultivated for irrigated coffee production before Kasama Coffee went into receivership in 2008, but the plantation is now moribund.

Assets include dry and wet processing facilities, warehouses, drip irrigation systems, employee housing, a recreational centre and a research centre.

The estate is expected to yield approximately 4,500 mt of arabica coffee beans per annum by 2021 when it is fully operational. The first 300 hectares are expected to be planted in 2013.

Supply and marketing chain. The company has strong and long-established relationships with its buyers. The firm attends seminars with the National Milling Company on meeting quality standards for wheat production.

The company sources inputs from local chemical companies: MRI Seed Limited, Greenbelt Fertilizer Company, Precision Farming and Crop Serve.

Exports. The company was not exporting in 2012 but Olam plans to export once production has been established.

Recent developments. In addition to producing wheat and soybeans, the firm has recently begun to prepare land in order to plant an initial 300 hectares of new coffee bushes.

Development agenda. The company plans to expand coffee production and increase the area under cultivation to 1,500 hectares in the next three years (from an initial 300 hectares that is being planted in 2012). It hopes to begin exporting to South Africa, Japan and America.

Olam International has pledged a further US$40 million of capital expenditure and preoperative expenditure to fully develop 2,000 hectares devoted to arabica coffee over the next five years.

Olam International plans to develop an area extending beyond the 1,580 hectares previously cultivated before Kasama Coffee went into receivership, eventually bringing a total of 2,000 hectares under production. This will translate into an output of approximately 4,500 mt of arabica coffee per annum at full yield.

4.2.10 Amigo Foods Limited

Basic details. Amigo Foods, a producer of snack foods, employs about 200 staff.

History. Amigo Foods is part of a larger group of companies that began with Sobi Industries, founded by the father of the current group managing director Soyeb Gheewala in 1972. Sobi Industries initially sold paper bags and from there diversified into making toilet paper. When the Zambian economy was liberalized, Mr Gheewala's father saw an opportunity to diversify production, and Amigo Foods was one of several companies he set up. The other companies in the group are Sobi Industries, which makes paper products, Plastex Packaging, which makes PET packaging, California Beverages, which makes soft drinks (see Chapter 5 on beverages), and Marydale Farm, which has a beef herd and cultivates wheat, maize, soya and potatoes.

Current activities and products. Amigo Foods manufactures a range of potato crisps and maize snacks.

Organization and management. The business is family run, with Soyeb Gheewala and his brother as managing directors for the whole group. Each company has a financial controller, a marketing manager, a purchasing department and a production manager.

Firm capabilities. The company produces 2,000 mt of potato crisps and maize snacks per annum.

Supply and marketing chain. Raw materials are 50–60% locally sourced and include maize ingredients supplied by the group's Marydale Farm. Oil is imported from South Africa, together with foil fresh packaging, which is not produced locally.

About 40% of its output is traded informally through local (street) markets. The company's potato crisp products compete effectively with imported brands on both price and quality, and account for about half of total sales of potato crisps in Zambia.

Exports. Exports account for about 6% of total output. Distribution sources have been established in Malawi and Zimbabwe. It is believed that a large part of sales to the informal sector go to small-scale operations abroad, particularly in the Democratic Republic of the Congo.

Chapter 5

BEVERAGES

5.1 Sector Profile

Background and overview. The non-alcoholic beverages sector comprises carbonated soft drinks, fruit juices, mineral water and maize-based drinks. (Milk is discussed in Chapter 4.)

The industrial manufacture of alcoholic beverages comprises spirits, clear beers and opaque beers. Clear beer is bought by more affluent consumers. Opaque beer sells at lower prices and is typically packaged in paper cartons.

Beverage manufacturers include

- large-scale industrial multinationals, dominated by Zambian Breweries, National Breweries and Varun Beverages;
- medium-sized firms making soft drinks, such as Californian Beverages;
- the larger opaque beer brewers;
- small-scale opaque beer brewers who deliver in bulk; and
- 'homebrew' micro enterprises making opaque beer and spirits in rural areas and in less affluent urban neighbourhoods.

Carbonated soft drinks. This segment is dominated by Coca-Cola and PepsiCo, and their Fanta, Sprite, Mirinda and Seven Up brands. These drinks are produced from concentrate, and are bottled both in (recycled) glass bottles and in plastic bottles by the local licence holders for distribution countrywide.

The long-established dominance in the market of Zambian Breweries, with its Coca-Cola franchise, has been eroded following the entry in 2001 of Varun Beverages, a PepsiCo franchisee.

A number of medium-sized companies, including Californian Beverages, have entered the market in recent years.

Juices. Most fruit juices are imported from South Africa, with some US$10.6 million imported in 2011, US$6.8 million in 2010 and US$7.6 million in 2009.[1] Fruit juices produced locally are generally made from imported concentrate. Parmalat and Californian Beverages are among the leading producers. Medium-sized juice and squash producers include Yaafico Industries Ltd, Fruitful Company Ltd, DK Enterprises Ltd and Lynx Zambia Ltd.

Water. The bottled mineral water market has become increasingly competitive in recent years, with the market leader, Natural Valley, facing competition from the entry of both international brands and small-scale producers. While Natural Valley continues to be the single largest bottled water company, with a market share of around a third, the market has become fragmented in the last 3–5 years, with between 50 and 60 new bottlers, led by Fairy Bottlers Ltd and Varun Beverages Zambia Ltd, entering the sector.

Maize-based drinks. Drinks based on a traditional process of adding a malting agent to maize porridge are a popular homemade drink. These have also been commercialized by companies such as Heinrich's Syndicate, which bought the market-leading Super Maheu No 1 brand from Trade Kings. Maheu is also produced by Yaafico.

Clear beer. Zambian Breweries is the only Zambia-based manufacturer of lager beer, producing under its Mosi and Castle brands. It produces Carling Black Label and Eagle beers under licence. Imported beers are growing in popularity.

Opaque beer. Opaque beer is a traditional beer made from sorghum and/or maize. National Breweries dominates the market with its Chibuku brand. This type of operation requires relatively low capital investment and expertise.

There are over 40 firms active in the opaque beer market. Opaque beer is sold in paper cartons rather than bottles. National Breweries and Midlands Breweries Limited sell exclusively in cartons. Chat Breweries, Central Breweries and Nkhosi Breweries Ltd sell both in cartons and in bulk, i.e. consumers fill their own containers from a large vat. National Breweries has an estimated market share of 65%. Smaller manufacturers sell direct to consumers from roadside bulk trucks.

[1] *Source*: http://comtrade.un.org/.

Supply and marketing chain. Flavourings and concentrates for soft drinks are imported, along with glass bottles. Hops and specialist yeasts are also imported.

Water, maize and, more recently, barley are bought locally.

Most firms using plastic bottles make these on site from preforms, while a few manufacture directly from imported granules. Varun has its own canning line, while National Breweries buys cartons from Nampak for its opaque beer.

The main manufacturers have well-established and efficient distribution networks countrywide.

Policy context. The excise tax on clear beer was reduced from 75% to 60% in 2009/10, and then to 40% in 2010/11.

In April 2012 the government banned the manufacture and sale of certain popular cheap strong spirits sold in small sachets ('tujilijili') due to alcohol abuse and health concerns.

Challenges. The industry is aware of environmental concerns about the use of plastic bottles, but this is tempered by the high cost of importing glass bottles.

Within the bottled water sector, quality standards are not always enforced by regulators, particularly for small firms.

Export status and potential. Varun has licensing rights to export Pepsi to neighboring countries and began exporting in 2012, although exports account for less than 10% of its sales. There is some informal border trade with the Democratic Republic of the Congo.

Profiles and lines of business of large firms.

Zambian Breweries, together with its sister companies **National Breweries** and **Heinrich's Syndicate**, are subsidiaries of SAB Miller. It bottles Coca-Cola and the main clear beers, as well as importing premium beers. It is profiled in the next section.

Invesco Ltd claims a 15–20% market share in carbonated soft drinks, and a 65% market share in cordials and water-based drinks. It is profiled in the next section.

Varun Beverages is a relatively new entrant but it has made significant investments and captured a sizable market share. It is profiled in the next section.

Californian Beverages, which is profiled in the next section, and **Acacia Beverages**, part of conglomerate Trade Kings, have strong carbonated soft drinks brands (Havana Cola, Flamingo) that have been developed locally.

Natural Valley has a dominant position in the mineral water market, despite increasing competition. The company is profiled in the next section.

Profiles and lines of business of medium-sized firms. While the Chibuku brand of National Breweries accounts for 65% of Zambian opaque beer sales, the remainder is manufactured by medium-sized and small firms such as Chat Breweries and Central Breweries, and at cottage-industry level.

Small-scale, informal and peripheral activities. Homebrew micro-industries are prolific throughout Zambia, making traditional opaque beer and Kachasu spirit (which is normally brewed from maize, although finger millet and various fruits are also used). Such unlicensed brewing is illegal in many areas under local bylaws. While drinking such brews is not banned, they have a high alcohol content and often pose threats to health.

5.2 Profiles of Major Firms

5.2.1 Zambian Breweries Plc

Basic details. Zambian Breweries and its sister company National Breweries Plc are Zambia's largest beverage companies. Both are majority-owned by the SAB Miller group of South Africa; they are listed on the Lusaka Stock Exchange as separate companies.

A third (wholly owned, unlisted) SAB Miller subsidiary, Heinrich's Syndicate Limited, makes a traditional flavoured maize drink under its Maheu brand.

Zambian Breweries reported turnover of US$236 million for the year 2012 and employs 1,100 people, while National Breweries reported US$50 million turnover in the same year and employs 560 staff. Heinrich's Syndicate employs 200 people.

History. South African Breweries expanded in Northern Rhodesia (now Zambia) in 1951 by opening a new brewery in Ndola. This was subsumed into Rhodesian Breweries Ltd when SAB Miller bought that company (Southern Rhodesia-based Rhodesian Breweries) a year later.

In 1963, in the run-up to independence, the operations were restructured and Northern Breweries Limited was incorporated, with South African Breweries owning 80% and Labatt Breweries of Canada 20%. Northern Breweries was nationalized in 1968, with the state-owned INDECO acquiring 55% from SAB Miller. SAB Miller's remaining 25% was sold to ZamAnglo Industrial Corporation Ltd, a subsidiary of the Anglo American Corporation.

In 1970 the company was renamed Zambia Breweries Limited. At that time it operated from two production facilities: one in Lusaka (Central Division) and one in Ndola (Northern Division).

In 1988 Labatt Breweries sold its 20% stake to INDECO and the company was renamed Zambian Breweries Limited.

As part of the government's 1990s privatization programme, the company's assets and liabilities were split into two newly incorporated companies. Central Division was transferred to Lusaka Breweries Limited while Northern Division became Northern Breweries (1995) Plc.

Lusaka Breweries Limited later changed its name to Zambian Breweries Plc and acquired the assets and liabilities of Central Division as well as the 'Mosi' trademark. In 1994 SAB Miller bought 45% of Zambian Breweries and assumed management control in 1994. In 1999 Zambian Breweries acquired 100% of the shares of Northern Breweries from Ugandan conglomerate the Madhavi Group, which bought Northern Breweries in 1997 from Lonrho Zambia Limited.[2]

The government acquired 51% of the shares in Heinrich's Syndicate in 1968, through INDECO, and renamed it National Breweries. In 1996 National Breweries was privatized, with 21% sold to Heinrich's Syndicate Limited bringing its shareholding to 70%. The remaining 30% of shares were offered to the public through the Zambia Privatisation Trust Fund. SAB Miller acquired 70% of National Breweries in 1999, with the remaining 30% floated on the Lusaka Stock Exchange in the same year.

In 2009 SAB Miller, through Heinrich's Syndicate Limited, bought the Maheu non-alcoholic flavoured maize drink business from Trade Kings for US$19.5 million.

Current activities and products. Zambian Breweries bottles Coca-Cola drinks and is the country's only manufacturer of clear beer. It has an 80%

[2] Lonrho Zambia Limited, the original purchaser on privatization in 1996, was required to sell Northern Breweries when Anglo American, which also had a stake in Zambian Breweries, purchased a stake in Lonrho (as the government had concerns about a lack of competition in the market).

market share in clear beer with its Mosi and Castle brands together with imported beers that it distributes.

Zambian Breweries is also licensed to produce mineral water under the Coca-Cola Company's Oasis brand but production is currently small.

National Breweries makes Chibuku brand opaque beer.

Organization and management. Zambian Breweries, National Breweries and Heinrich's Syndicate Limited are separate companies but share integrated support services, with one managing director responsible for all three businesses.

SAB Miller owns 84% of Zambian Breweries, 76% of National Breweries and 100% of Heinrich's Syndicate Limited.

Firm capabilities. Zambian Breweries has an annual production capacity of 750,000 hectolitres at its Lusaka plant and 300,000 hectolitres in Ndola, producing Mosi, Mosi Gold, Castle lager, Carling Black Label and Eagle beer, as well as Coca-Cola brand soft drinks.

It operates above its rated capacity, producing 1.1 million hectolitres of clear beer and 560,000 hectolitres of soft drinks in 2011. It also imports some beers, including Castle Lite, Miller, Peroni and Black Label.

National Breweries operates manufacturing plants in Kitwe, Ndola, Kabwe, Lusaka and Chipata. Plants need to be close to consumers due to the short shelf life of opaque beer. It produced 1.7 million hectolitres of Chibuku in 2011 and is working close to full capacity.

Heinrich's Syndicate Limited produced 300,000 hectolitres of its Maheu spirit.

Supply and marketing chain. Malted barley was imported from South Africa and Europe until 2011, when a programme of local cultivation came on stream. The crop is exported to Zimbabwe for malting and then returned to Zambia. As of 2012 it expects to have a surplus of barley for export.

Maize is bought locally, while hops and yeast are imported.

Glass bottles are imported from the Middle East and South Africa, with labels and crown closures supplied locally by Nampak.

Soft drink concentrates are imported from Swaziland, sugar is bought from Zambia Sugar and glass bottles are recycled. Preform PET bottles are imported from South Africa. Sorghum is sourced locally for the manufacture of Eagle beer.

National Breweries buys maize and sorghum locally.

Zambian Breweries does about 20% of its own distribution, with the rest being handled by a network of distributors. National Breweries has a similar network, but does slightly more direct distribution.

Recent developments. Construction started in 2011 on a new US$90 million brewery in Ndola with an annual production capacity of 1 million hectolitres of clear beer.

A PET line for Chibuku, which will extend its product's shelf life, was being commissioned in October 2012.

Development agenda. Zambian Breweries is investigating the feasibility of a malting plant.

5.2.2 Varun Beverages (Zambia) Limited

Basic details. Varun Beverages (Zambia) is a new entrant into the Zambian beverages sector. It bottles PepsiCo products and Aquaclear mineral water. It has an annual turnover of approximately US$25million, of which less than 10% comes from exports. The company has 500 staff.

History. Varun Beverages (Zambia) is wholly owned by the India conglomerate RJ Corporation. Having established operations in Uganda, Kenya and then Mozambique, the group set up its business in Zambia in 2009 as a greenfield operation with an investment licence from the Zambia Development Agency, land allocated by the government, and a concession to defer payment of value-added tax (VAT) for five years, on the basis of a pledge to invest US$25 million over six years. Factory construction began in the same year, with operations starting in 2010.

Current activities and products. Current production is 15.15 million 24-bottle cases of carbonated soft drinks per annum, 2 million cases of juices per annum, and 5.15 million cases of mineral water per annum. Output grew by 25% in 2012, with growth forecast at around 10% per year.

The company has four production lines: water, at a capacity of 5,000 bottles per hour; glass bottles, at 500 bottles per minute; PET plastic bottles, at 200 per minute; and cans, at 400 per minute. It has the only operational beverage canning line in the country.

It has about 20% of the carbonated soft drinks market. Some 70% of its drinks are sold in glass bottles.

Organization and management. The local board of directors is headed by the CEO. Senior management includes a vice president of sales and marketing, and managers responsible for territory development and management information systems.

Firm capabilities. The company has rights to bottle PepsiCo products (including Pepsi, Mirinda and Seven Up) in Zambia and to export to neighbouring countries.

The company supplies crates to distributors. It can make 2,000 crates per day, and some 200,000 have so far been distributed to retailers without payment of a deposit; this move which was a key element in the company's penetration of the market.

The company has laboratory testing facilities and an effluent treatment plant.

Supply and marketing chain. Varun Beverages (Zambia) imports PepsiCo brand concentrates, from which it makes syrups.

Preform plastic bottles, cans and plastic granules for the manufacture of crates are imported from South Africa.

The company has 140 distributors countrywide, to whom it delivers using a mix of company-owned and hired trucks.

Exports. The firm has recently started exporting beverages—mainly Pepsi—to Zimbabwe, Malawi and the Democratic Republic of the Congo. Export sales account for less than 10% of turnover. It may in the future begin bottling in these countries.

Development agenda. The company plans to start a US$15 million dairy operation in 2013, producing ice cream, flavoured milk and yoghurt. It will initially use imported powdered milk, but it plans to gradually move to local purchasing of fresh milk.

The company also plans to add a beer brewing operation.

5.2.3 Californian Beverages

Basic details. Californian Beverages is a registered partnership between four Zambians of Asian descent: Younus Suleman, Hemant Salvi, Ismail Gheewala and Soyeb Gheewala. The company is located in the main industrial area of Lusaka. Apart from the multinational companies that distribute Coca-Cola and Pepsi, it is the largest distributor and manufacturer of soft drinks in the country. The company employs 350 full-time staff, as well as casual workers.

History. The company was registered in 2001 by the four partners after they came up with the idea of manufacturing health drinks from local fruits. At the time, there was no other domestic company producing soft drinks except for Zambian Bottlers (Coca-Cola).

The four partners saw a gap in the market for real fruit juices, and registered the company to produce and market them as health drinks.

Current activities and products. The company produces 17 different types of drink under three categories.

- Ready to drink and mixers: Apple Max, Hubbly Bubbly, Tingling Ginger Beer, California Fruity, Cali Cola, Sweet Lemon, Sweet Nutch, Sweet Mix Berry.
- Squashes: orange, pineapple and granadilla.
- Cordials: orange, pineapple, raspberry, cream soda and blackcurrant.

It produces an estimated 20 million litres of drinks per annum.

Supply and marketing chain. The company has over 100 suppliers across the country. Californian Beverages has a customer base of over 2,000 bulk buyers to whom it delivers directly. Its location in the main industrial part of the city is convenient for industrial customers. It supplies vendors that work from kiosks throughout the country.

The company advertises heavily on television, in newspapers and through sponsored events. It has distribution points in nine provinces.

Competition. For some years, California Beverages enjoyed a high market share as the only company producing health fruit drinks. However, over the years other companies have begun to produce similar drinks. While these rivals are small individually, they jointly constitute a strong competitive fringe in the industry. There is also competition in this area from imported drinks, but California Beverages prices its products slightly lower than imported alternatives.

Organization and management. One of the four partners, Hemant Salvi, acts as operations manager in Lusaka and holds regular meetings with the other partners on planning and operational decision making.

Challenges. The firm's major challenge is the lack of land for expansion. The plot it operates on has become too small over the years. However, to overcome this, Californian Beverages is now building a two-storey structure on its site to create office space and storage facilities. Some of its packaging is sourced from abroad due to the lack of availability of appropriate supplies on the local market.

Development agenda. The company plans to export to the Southern African region once its expansion process is completed.

Exports. Californian Beverages exports small quantities to Malawi, Tanzania and the Democratic Republic of the Congo.

5.2.4 Natural Valley Limited

Basic details. Natural Valley, under its registered brand name Manzi Valley, is Zambia's largest producer of bottled mineral water. It employs up to 180 people, peaking in the hot season. Its annual turnover is US$5 million.

History. Natural Valley was incorporated in 2000, supported by a loan from the joint Nordic/Southern African Development Community (NORSAD) initiative, and set up a plant in Chongwe on the outskirts of Lusaka.

The company was set up by the current owner's father and was the first company to produce bottled water in Zambia.

Current activities and products. Natural Valley bottles mineral water in sizes ranging from 500 ml to 20 l from its factory in Chongwe on the outskirts of Lusaka.

The company has also diversified into transport services.

Organization and management. Natural Valley is a family-owned company run by a husband and wife team as directors, with four middle managers.

Firm capabilities. The market demand for mineral water in Zambia is estimated at 50–55 million litres per year, of which Natural Valley produces 15.5 million litres. It is certified by the ZABS.

Supply and marketing chain. Some 40% of PET bottles are produced in-house using granules from South Africa. Labels are imported from Zimbabwe.

The company has 28 vehicles and distributes countrywide. Supermarket chain stores account for 20% of sales, as compared with 10% five years ago.

Competition. While the total market for mineral water is growing, so too is supply, with the industry becoming increasingly competitive in recent years. (There are now 50–60 producers, but quality standards are not enforced.)

Natural Valley's sales have been growing by around 5% a year in the last 3–5 years, a slower rate of growth than the 15% growth it achieved before new firms entered the market.

Natural Valley has a market share of 34–35%. Its nearest competitor is Fairy Bottling Zambia Limited, with its Aquasavana brand, which began operations in 2007 and has an estimated market share of 15%. Varun Beverages (Zambia) Limited, with its Aquaclear brand, has an estimated share of 10%. It began operations in 2010.

Recent developments. The installation in 2012 of an integrated management information system is enhancing the company's ability to market strategically.

Development agenda. The company plans to invest in larger bottling machines when financial resources permit.

5.2.5 Invesco Limited

Basic details. Invesco trading as Goldspot Bottling Company, makes carbonated soft drinks and still cordials and juices. Turnover is projected at US$36 million in 2012, 10% of which comes from exports. The company employs 420 full-time staff.

History. The business was started by the current managing director Ajesh Patel's Indian grandparents, who settled in Livingstone in 1927. Mr Patel's grandfather made sweets from sesame seed. His grandmother's family traded garments, mostly second-hand clothes imported from the UK. As it expanded, the business followed the development of the railway line to the Copperbelt. Later, it began to manufacture copper-based fungicides. With the rise in copper prices, that business became relatively unprofitable, however, and it was decided to focus the business on food, beverages and confectionery. Invesco was one of the first beverage companies in the Central African region to manufacture, fill and package its products in PET bottles. PET bottles are blown at Invesco's Ndola factory.

Invesco was incorporated in 1991, when it began production under a franchise agreement with Parle Exports Private Limited, a major Indian food and beverage company, to manufacture and distribute Parle's brands of carbonated drinks Thums Up, Limca, Citra and Goldspot in Zambia. The Coca-Cola Company subsequently purchased these brands, and Invesco continued production of Limca, Citra and Goldspot under the authority of the Coca-Cola Company, operating under a standard international bottler's agreement.

Current activities and products. Invesco has increased its blowing and filling capacity and has been authorized to manufacture additional Coca-Cola and Schweppes brands including Coca-Cola, Coke Light, Fanta, Sprite and the Kinley range of mixers. It also produces local cordials and manufactures its own range of carbonated drinks under the Fiesta brand, which includes ginger beer and Crystal brand water.

Organization and management. The business remains a family-owned and run business, though British American Tobacco Plc has a minority (40%) stake. Expatriate experts are occasionally hired to assist in marketing operations and installing information technology systems.

Competition and market share. Invesco has two product lines: carbonated soft drinks and still cordials and juices. It has a 15–20% market share in carbonated soft drinks and a share of about 65% in cordials and water-based drinks.

Supply and marketing chain. Sugar is sourced locally from Zambia Sugar, and PET resin is imported from South Africa, Nigeria and Zimbabwe. Concentrates for juices, drinks and cordials come from Coca-Cola in Swaziland. Packaging materials are sourced locally. The final products are distributed through wholesale distributors to supermarket outlets (Shoprite, Pick n Pay and Spar). There are separate channels for distribution to the informal market, in smaller case sizes.

Exports. About 10% of total production is exported, with 60% of this going to the Democratic Republic of the Congo, 30% to Malawi and 10% to Zimbabwe.

In Zimbabwe, wholesale deliveries are made to buyers' depots. In Malawi, Invesco uses the Coca-Cola network for distribution. Exports to the Democratic Republic of the Congo are largely informal: Congolese wholesalers purchase stock from the Ndola headquarters.

Recent developments. Invesco is currently in the process of investing in citrus fruit distilling technology, to take advantage of the growing middle-class market in the country. It plans to source fruit from local outgrower schemes.

Invesco is considering a US$2.2 million investment in new technology, aimed at increasing the shelf life of bottles from 12 weeks to 12 months. It is also exploring the viability of purchasing a biodegradable packaging plant.

Chapter 6

COTTON

6.1 Sector Profile

Background and overview. Zambia's climatic conditions and soil type are generally good for cotton production, yet of over 800,000 hectares of potential land, only about 300,000 hectares is currently under cotton cultivation. Cotton is produced by over 150,000 small-scale farmers under outgrower contracts with ginning companies. Cotton lint consumption by Zambia's spinning industry is approximately 14,500 mt per annum, while local lint production of 72,000 mt exceeds local demand.[1]

The once-thriving Zambian textile industry has been decimated by the importation of cheap 'salaula' second-hand clothes. Cotton ginners are operating well below capacity and are exporting virtually all of their production rather than selling to the domestic textile industry.

Zambia is, therefore, basically a raw cotton exporter; it was ranked 24th in world cotton exports in 2007. Raw cotton exports have been increasing in the last ten years, from about US$5 million in 2000 to a high of US$122 million in 2004. They currently stand at around US$30 million per annum. Raw cotton is exported to South Africa, Mauritius and East Asia.

The cotton sector was run by a parastatal company called Lint Company of Zambia (LINTCO) between 1979 and 1994. Prior to that period, trade was informal. When LINTCO was established in 1979, production was fluctuating but low, at 30,000 mt per annum, with participation from around 30,000 outgrowers.[2] LINTCO was then sold to Lonrho Cotton and Clark Cotton,[3] two private companies with regional cotton interests, with each introducing its own outgrower scheme. Since privatization,

[1] Zambia Development Agency. 2011. *Agriculture, Livestock and Fisheries: Sector Profile* (February).

[2] Kabwe, S. 2009. The evolution of the cotton and textile industry in Zambia. Food Security Research Project, unpublished presentation (April).

[3] Tschirley, D., and S. Kabwe. 2010. A case study of regulation in Zambia's cotton sector. Food Security Research Project, Working Paper 45 (April).

TABLE 6.1. The ginning capacities of the major cotton companies in Zambia.

Company	Location	Capacity (mt per season)
Dunavant	Kabwe	25,000
	Mumbwa	25,000
	Gwembe	24,000
	Sinazongwe	10,000
	Lundazi	18,000
	Katete	28,000
Cargill Zambia	Chipata	60,000
Alliance Cotton	Kafue	24,000
Continental	Sinda	18,000
	Kalomo	6,000
Mulungushi	Kabwe	10,000
Chipata China Cotton	Chipata	80,000
Total		328,000

cotton prices are set by the market. Initially, four new ginning companies emerged together with smaller, independent traders. Today the cotton industry is dominated by foreign-owned companies; it contributes around US$60–70 million to the economy annually.

Profiles and lines of business of large firms. Dunavant is the largest cotton ginner in Zambia, followed by Cargill, Alliance Ginneries, Olam International and Continental Ginneries. The Chinese-backed Chipata Cotton Company is smaller but growing. Another Chinese company, AST, a new entrant in the 2011/12 season, uses ginning facilities provided on a toll basis by Yustina, a small-scale Malawian company with a gin in Chipata.

The ginning industry is dominated by a handful of large multinational companies. With the exception of the Alliance Ginneries gin at Kafue, most of the gins are well established and their capital cost has been fully depreciated (Table 6.1).

Dunavant. A number of companies have entered the ginning market since 2006/7, and Dunavant's market share has declined from nearly 60% to 41% since that time. Dunavant is profiled in the next section.

Cargill Zambia Limited. Cargill Zambia is the second largest ginnery in the country after Dunavant. It is profiled in the next section.

Profiles and lines of business of medium-sized firms.

Alliance Ginneries Limited. Alliance Ginneries is a major multinational cotton processor that entered the Zambian market in 2007. It is profiled in the next section.

Continental Ginnery Ltd. Continental Ginnery is owned by an Indo-Zimbabwean company, Parrogate, and operates two gins: a saw gin in Sinda and a roller gin in Kalomo. In 2008 it began producing cotton seed oil and marketing this under its White Gold label. Its machine has a capacity of 60 mt a day and an extraction rate of 12%. Most of its lint is exported through Olam Zambia Ltd.

Mulungushi Cotton and Cooking Oil Ltd. Mulungushi Cotton and Cooking Oil formerly bought seed cotton, ginned it and sold it to its parent company, Zambia-China Mulungushi Textiles Ltd, which has now closed down. Currently, Mulungushi Cotton and Cooking Oil buys cotton, gins it and exports the lint to China directly.

Olam Zambia. Olam, the third largest global cotton company, is a relatively new entrant to Zambia. Its business model is different to that of its main competitors, in that it has taken advantage of excess capacity in the ginning industry to outsource ginning. It has a contract with Continental Ginneries. In 2007/8 Olam sourced cotton from 12,000 farmers and produced 5,000 mt of seed cotton. It currently has 21,000 outgrowers and is expected to produce 13,000–14,000 mt. It operates in the Nyimba area of Eastern Province.

Small-scale, informal and peripheral activities. A handful of new, mostly Chinese, companies entered the market in 2012. However, cotton prices are currently low and, in the absence of government support in terms of input supply and extension services, small-scale growers are increasingly diversifying into other activities.

Supply and marketing chain. All ginneries produce ginned cotton and cottonseed. Some also process the cottonseed to produce cottonseed oil and cottonseed cake.

Export status and potential. In the 2009 budget, the Zambian government increased income tax on the profit earned from exporting cotton lint from 15% to 35%. Concessions may be offered, however, if an export permit is obtained from the Ministry of Commerce, Trade and Industry and local capacity has already been met for any particular season. The export levy on lint and fuzzy seed, a stockfeed export to South Africa, was also increased from 15% to 20%, and the corporate tax rate on exported lint was increased from 15% to the standard 35%.

Cottonseed oil competes with other food oils, so the recent removal of import duty on palm oil in the 2009 budget, which is relatively cheap, has had the effect of reducing the returns to producers of cottonseed oil.

Exports. Zambia was ranked 24th in world cotton exports in 2007. Raw cotton exports have increased from about US$5 million in 2000 to as high as US$122 million in 2004; they are currently around US$30 million per annum. Raw cotton from Zambia is sold mainly to South Africa, Mauritius and East Asia.[4]

Zambia's output represents less than 1% of world market demand for cotton.

Policy context. The government retains the right, through the introduction of a 'statutory instrument', to influence or manage the price of cotton. However, it has chosen instead to leave the market to determine the price. The private sector sets prices and marketing arrangements and has almost exclusive access to policy discussions and formulation. There is some frustration within the industry at the perceived reluctance of the government to boost production, particularly through the implementation of robust input supply programmes and extension services for small-scale outgrowers.

Competitiveness. Zambia produces medium staple cotton (a medium grade of cotton based on the length of its fibres) that would be used locally in greater quantities if investment was made in setting up spinning mills or integrated textile mills. Currently, it is used predominantly in the manufacture of uniforms and protective clothing.

Challenges. The gins in Zambia are operating significantly below capacity. The market price for cotton yarn is highly variable and this variability is made worse by the volatility of the ZMK/US$ exchange rate.

6.2 Profiles of Major Firms

6.2.1 Dunavant Zambia Ltd

Basic details. Dunavant Zambia—part of the US-based Dunavant Enterprises Inc, the largest privately owned cotton trader in the world—is

[4] Zambia Development Agency, Agriculture Sector Profile, February 2011.

Zambia's largest cotton ginner. All of its cotton lint, around 220,000 mt in 2012, is exported.

The company was owned, up to December 2012, by a private holding company in Switzerland (through an intermediary African holding company) that has operations worldwide. In December 2012, NWK of Lichtenburg acquired a 60% interest in Dunavant Zambia via its parent company AfricaNeth Coöperatif UA, which is based in the Netherlands. The remaining 40% of Dunavant Zambia's equity will be taken up by Louis Dreyfus Commodities.

History. Dunavant Zambia's operations began as the government-owned Lint Company of Zambia, set up by the government in 1976 to develop the country's cotton industry. LINTCO's assets were sold to Lonrho Africa and Clark Cotton in 1995. Dunavant purchased the assets from Lonrho in 2000.

Current activities and products. Dunavant Zambia's head office is in Lusaka, and it owns ginneries in Kabwe and Mumbwa (Central Province), Gwembe (Southern Province), and Katete and Lundazi (Eastern Province). A mill in Sinazongwe was acquired in 2011 from Great Lakes Cotton Company following the company's liquidation, but it was closed in 2012, along with a mill in Petauke. The ginneries have a total capacity of 112,000 mt.

The company buys raw cotton from a network of farmers—169,000 in the 2011/12 season—to which it provides seeds, chemicals and fertilizer on credit, as well as training services.

The raw cotton is ginned into lint. Cooking oil is produced from cotton seed at the Katete plant and is then sold through a wholly owned subsidiary, Dunavant Oils Zambia Limited, in both the domestic and export markets. The oil business represents a little less than 10% of Dunavant's turnover.

Cotton seed cake is sold as animal feed, and cotton hulls are used for chicken bedding.

Organization and management. The company is run by a professional management team in Lusaka that has autonomy over day-to-day operations. The team is headed by a managing director, who has a board of directors, comprising local and overseas non-executives, the manager of Dunavant Oils and the Katete plant manager, under him.

Firm capabilities. The firm has sufficient capacity to gin 112,000 mt of raw cotton a year, but it was operating at only 50–60% capacity during 2012.

Supply and marketing chain. Dunavant Zambia's base of smallholder farmer outgrowers is central to its operations. The company sources seed, chemicals and a small amount of fertilizer through a tender process and supplies to these farmers on credit. Costs are then deducted from the final sale price of the raw cotton. Loan recovery rates are generally more than 90%. The industry was estimated to have extended approximately US$18 million of inputs on credit for 2011/12.

The company runs a training scheme, partly funded by the Gates Foundation and the German development agency Deutsche Investitions- und Entwicklungsgesellschaft.

The Zambia Cotton Ginners Association introduced a collective agreement in 2010/11 with the Cotton Association of Zambia, which acts on behalf of farmers. The agreement provides for a fixed price to be offered to farmers by ginners and was introduced in an attempt to prevent 'side-buying' by buyers who had not provided inputs. (See Chapter 4 for a discussion of 'side-buying'.)

Output doubled to 140,000 mt in 2010/11, rising again in 2011/12 to 220,000 mt on the back of the price increase, but a drop was expected by ginners for the 2012/13 season.

Transporters are also important suppliers, with trucking services outsourced for distribution of inputs, collection of raw cotton and shipping of lint.

Exports. All of Dunavant Zambia's lint production is exported, mainly to customers in the Far East, who are found by the parent company's Geneva trading desk.

The liquidation of Swarp Spinning Mill in 2008 (see p. 81) meant the closure of Dunavant's only local buyer, which had accounted for a small proportion of its sales.

Recent developments. In recent years Dunavant Zambia has diversified into the trading of maize and soybean, and it has also opened two retail centres, in Petauke and Katete, to supply farmers with roofing sheets, solar panels and animal feed.

Development agenda. The company plans to add further retail outlets and expand its crop trading activities to include sorghum and cowpeas, thus providing a market for farmers and encouraging crop rotation, which improves cotton yields.

6.2.2 Cargill Zambia Limited

Basic details. Cargill is an international producer and marketer of food, agricultural, financial and industrial products and services. The company employs 850 permanent staff in Zambia, as well as 1,000 seasonal workers.

History. Founded in 1865, Cargill is a privately held company that employs 142,000 people in 65 countries. Cargill was established in Zambia in 2006, when it acquired the business of Clark Cotton Zambia Ltd from Afgri Corporation Ltd, a South African agribusiness company, as part of a wider purchase of Afgri's cotton ginning business in Southern Africa.

Clark Cotton was previously a division of the South African food company Premier Food Industries, and it bought some of the assets of the former state-owned cotton company LINTCO in 1995. Premier sold its Southern African cotton business, Clark Cotton Pty Ltd, to South African agribusiness OTK Holdings Ltd in 1999, and then OTK was renamed Afgri in 2003.

In 2008 Cargill opened its first grain and oilseed trading office in the region and production was initiated that year.

Current activities and products. Cargill has activities in cotton growing and ginning as well as grain and oilseed cultivating and trading. Cargill also provides inputs such as seed, fertilizer and pesticides on credit to cotton, grain and oilseed farmers, which in many cases enables them to continue to grow their produce year on year. Through long-term relationships with cotton farmers, Cargill prides itself on supporting programmes that improve agricultural practices, provide essential financial and technical support, offer better access to crop inputs and help farmers increase their incomes.

Organization and management. Cargill's Zambian operation is part of the Middle East and African business, which also involves operations in South Africa, Egypt, Morocco and Kenya.

Firm capabilities. Cargill Zambia has a ginning capacity of around 60,000 mt per season and is the second largest ginnery in the country after Dunavant.

Supply and marketing chain. Cargill supports cotton farmers through programmes such as Cotton Made in Africa, of which Cargill became a partner in 2012. The project provides farmers with improved market access and ensures that cotton is produced using good agricultural and environmental practices.

Exports. The lint produced is exported through South Africa and is mostly shipped to markets in the Far East.

Recent developments. The Competitive African Cotton Initiative (COMPACI) is a three-year programme that aims to strengthen the cotton production capacities of participating farmers in sub-Saharan Africa. In December 2009 Cargill and others in the cotton sector joined two German international development organizations (Deutsche Investitions- und Entwicklungsgesellschaft and the German Organisation for Technical Cooperation), the Bill and Melinda Gates Foundation and the German Federal Ministry for Economic Cooperation and Development to implement and support a programme to provide assistance to 265,000 farmers in sub-Saharan Africa.

By increasing productivity and competitiveness, the COMPACI program aims to grow the incomes of small-scale farmers in the Eastern Province of Zambia by at least 34% over three years. In 2010 Cargill worked with over 42,800 farmers, of which around 26,000 participated in the COMPACI project. In 2011 Cargill aims to work with 65,000 farmers under the scheme.

Cargill has established a network of 560 training schools across the region to teach cotton farmers agricultural and environmentally sustainable practices.

Cargill joined the Southern Africa Soy Value Chain Development Program in November 2010, working with Technoserve to support the programme in Zambia. The objective of this programme is to boost the annual incomes of 37,000 smallholder farmers in Mozambique and Zambia by US$200 within four years.

6.2.3 Alliance Ginneries Limited

Basic details. Alliance Ginneries is a multinational organization that buys, processes and markets cotton. It operates ginneries and oil plants in Kenya, Tanzania, Zambia and Zimbabwe. Alliance Ginneries bought 12,500,000 kg of cotton in 2010/11 and its turnover that year was US$14.6 million, with exports valued at US$14.3 million. Alliance Ginneries employs 120 full-time staff, with an extra 500–1,500 employees taken on during peak times.

History. Alliance Ginneries Limited was founded when Alliance Ginneries entered the market from Kenya in 2007. The firm was founded in Kenya, where Munir Zaveri's grandfather settled in 1895, having emigrated from a cotton-producing region of India. He began trading textiles and garments 1904 and built a ginnery in Kenya in 1935. The ginnery was operated as a family business until the 1990s. The family decided to move its Alliance Ginneries business out of Kenya and began production in Zimbabwe in 2004, before coming to Zambia in 2007. The family still lives in Kenya.

Current activities and products. The company contracts around 40,000 small-scale outgrowers from its base in Kafue outside Lusaka to produce medium staple cotton that is rolled into bales wrapped in plastic sheeting for export. The seed cotton is purchased from the farmer at harvest time and then processed into lint. The cotton is ginned to separate the fibre from the seed and then bailed.

Organization and management. The firm's headquarters are in Nairobi, Kenya, which is where the founding family members live and manage the parent company. In Zambia the business is run by two directors, a general manager and technical staff at the factory in Kafue. The company also has regional managers and area managers who control distribution.

Firm capabilities. The firm has a fully integrated cotton ginning process; it uses a mix of American and Indian machinery and equipment. Alliance Ginneries accounts for about 8% of industry output, its main competitors being Dunavant and Cargill.

Supply and marketing chain. Small-scale growers are given input packages (seed, pesticides and fertilizer) as a loan, which the grower repays at harvest time. The farmers are then legally obliged to sell an agreed amount of their harvest to Alliance Ginneries. The farmer is free to sell any surplus elsewhere. Alliance Ginneries contracts around 40,000 farmers, with typical plots of about 2 hectares. The firm has a few direct contracts with companies in South Africa, but it mostly sells to trading merchants in Europe.

Exports. Most of its cotton is exported. Generally, Zambia's medium staple cotton is of a higher grade than can be used in Zambia due to limited manufacturing capacity; the only local use is in the manufacture of uniforms and protective wear.

Recent developments. In light of current challenges surrounding the low price of cotton, the company is shifting its focus to boosting mechanized production, improving extension services, and hiring an agronomist to increase yields.

Chapter 7

TEXTILES, GARMENTS AND LEATHER

7.1 Sector Profile: Textiles and Garments

Background and overview. The textiles and leather sector contributed around US$1.9 million, or 0.25%, to Zambia's GDP in 2010.[1]

The textile, garments and leather sector has been in decline in recent years. The country's only cotton spinning mill, Swarp Milling, closed down in 2009. This has had a negative impact on the weaving, knitting and garments sector.

Cheap imported second-hand clothes, 'salaula', have decimated Zambia's conventional garment industry. It now largely focuses on school uniforms and workwear, often produced under contracts from government and large companies such as mining firms.

In the 1990s there were 150 clothing factories in the country but now there are reportedly only five.

Most of the Zambian army's uniforms are currently produced in China, while Kenya supplies uniforms to the Zambia Police Service.

The remaining domestic weaving, knitting and garment producers mostly work with obsolete machinery, producing poor-quality output for the domestic market.

Spinning. Zambia's spinning capacity reached its peak output, of 23,500 mt, in 1997, when it had six spinning mills, none of which are now operational. Until 2009, the exception was Swarp Milling, which had relatively new equipment and an annual capacity of 14,000 mt. Swarp spun virtually all the lint in Zambia that was not exported and supplied yarn to domestic weavers and knitters. Domestic spinners processed around 20,000 mt, or 7%, of Zambia's lint in 2007/8.[2] Around 30% of Zambia's lint was sold locally, 40% was exported to South Africa, 20% to the EU and 10% to the Far East.

[1] Central Statistical Office. 2001. *The Monthly* (November).

[2] Cotton Development Trust. 2008.*Zambia Country Report to the 67th ICAC Plenary Meeting, Burkina Faso* (November).

Spinners agreed pre-season prices with ginners based on the Liverpool A Index charged on an import parity basis including freight charges, thus making the price expensive for spinners and possibly contributing to their demise. For example, in 2003 Swarp paid US$1.20 per kg for imported lint and US$1.24 per kg for local lint, and the factory gate price of its cotton yarn was US$2 per kg. At the height of production, spinners imported about 2,000 mt per annum of lint with a longer staple from Zimbabwe to blend with local cotton.[3]

Despite having orders going through to August 2009, Swarp was put into receivership in December 2008 by its creditors (the CDC, PTA Bank and the African Development Bank).

There are other spinning mills in Zambia, but none of these are operational. They include the old and mothballed Mukuba Textiles in Ndola with an annual capacity of 1,200 mt; Thonje (formerly Starflex) in Ndola with an annual capacity of 1,200 mt, which has been broken up and sold; Excel in Ndola (1,650 mt), which is not operational; Mulungushi in Kabwe (3,000 mt), which is currently closed; African Textiles (formerly Kafue Textiles) of Kafue (3,000 mt); and a number of small spinners, mostly in the Copperbelt, with a combined annual capacity of 1,000 mt.[4] Total capacity was around 23,750 mt, but it should be noted that capacity estimates vary.

Weaving, knitting and dyeing. Most of the country's weaving and knitting companies have now closed. Those still operating in 2009 included Kay's Textiles (Ndola), Mukuba Textiles (Ndola), African Textiles (Kafue), Excel Textiles (Ndola) and Markweld (Lusaka).

Cut–make–trim. The cut–make–trim industry is largely confined to production of workwear and uniforms.

Around US$3–4 million of garments are made and sold in Zambia each year using fabric that is around 95% imported. Local textile producers make mutton cloth for the mines using yarn imported from India.

Profiles and lines of business of large firms.

Unity Garments. Unity Garments is part of the Unity group of companies based in Ndola; it is the largest garment manufacturer in Zambia and is profiled in the next section.

[3] Regional Agricultural Trade Expansion Support Program. 2003. *Cotton-Textile-Apparel Value Chain Report Zambia* (August).

[4] Tschirley, D., and S. Kabwe. 2007. *Cotton in Zambia: 2007 Assessment of its Organisation, Performance, Current Policy Initiatives and Challenges for the Future* (September). Food Security Research Project.

Zamleather. Zamleather is the only leather tannery in the country that operates at capacity. It is profiled in the next section.

Medium-sized firms in clothing. The textiles and garments industry is dominated by medium-sized firms, often operating with outmoded equipment.

Amalgamated Dress Zambia Limited. Amalgamated Dress is based in Ndola. It was established in 1976 and started making overalls for the then-government-owned Zambia Consolidated Copper Mines before expanding into industrial uniforms in the 1980s.

Caress Lingerie Limited. Caress Lingerie, based in Ndola, manufactures underwear.

Central Clothing Factory Limited. Lusaka-based Central Clothing Factory (garments) and its sister companies Vimal Textiles Limited (weaving) and Zambia Knitting (knitting) undertake weaving and knitting as well as making workwear. Its products are sold domestically and in the Democratic Republic of the Congo.

City Clothing Factory. The company makes mainly workwear and school uniforms, selling through tendered contracts or through its own store.

It employs 70 labourers and three designers and has 55–60 sewing machines. It operates at near full capacity (80–90%), with weekend shifts included.

City Clothing Factory buys around 100,000–120,000 m of fabric per annum, of which around half is cotton and the rest polyester/polycotton. About half the fabric it buys in is manufactured locally and the remainder comes from importers. It has problems with the quality of bought-in fabric, with inconsistent dyeing shades.

Kay's Textiles Limited. Kay's Textiles produces bed sheets and some workwear and uniforms for the domestic market. Its machines are old and slow and manufacturing times are long; management has considered whether to invest in up-to-date machinery. The factory finds it hard to compete with cheap imports.

Mukuba Textiles. Mukuba Textiles of Ndola has a spinning capacity of 130 mt per month, with direct manual feed. As of 2009 it was mothballed except for the occasional contract spinning of heavy yarn for tarpaulins for nearby Excel Textiles.

TABLE 7.1. Textile and garment export earnings by sector, 2005–10 (all figures in thousands of US$).

	2005	2006	2007	2008	2009	2010
Textiles	26,937	19,584	15,222	18,518	4,779	1,951
Garments	445	315	7,177	8,083	944	506
Total	29,387	21,905	24,406	28,609	7,732	4,467

Source: Exporter Audit Report 2010, Zambia Development Agency.

Markweld. Markweld believes it can sell 200 mt of fabric per annum if it purchases faster machines, and it plans to acquire UK sales connections to help it with marketing.

Tribal Textiles. Tribal Textiles was founded in 1991 by a British woman. It employs more than 100 people in the Luangwa Valley making high-quality cotton items such as bags, cushion covers and aprons with striking, original designs aimed mostly at the international tourist market. Its uniqueness is based on its deigns, which are hand-painted onto fabrics. The factory has its own shop, selling to tourists.

Small-scale, informal and peripheral activities. Cottage industry operations exist in most townships, often comprising one former clothing factory worker with his or her own sewing machine, making school uniforms and other clothing to order.

Zambia has a number of talented individual fashion designers operating on a 'bespoke' couture basis, making their living largely from the custom wedding dress market. Their creativity can be impressive, but they lack the resources to mass produce garments on a commercial basis.

Supply and marketing chain. Most of Zambia's textiles are imported from India and China.

Garment manufacturers rely on contracts with mining firms and other industries to supply workwear.

Export status and potential. Textiles accounted for US$1.95 million of exports in 2010, while garments accounted for US$0.5 million.

Exports declined by 93% between 2005, when they totalled US$27 million, and 2010, when they were less than US$2 million. Garment exports have remained more resilient, with a significant peak in 2007 and 2008 (Table 7.1).[5]

[5] Zambia Development Agency. 2010. *Exporter Audit Report 2010.*

Policy context. Garment manufacturers are currently lobbying for government to require all uniforms in Zambia—for the military, for schools, for hospitals and for the police—to be sourced from local producers for three years. They estimate this could create 10,000 jobs and provide economies of scale that would encourage component manufacturers to start businesses.

There are also calls for a duty to be established on imported second-hand clothes, which would help to establish confidence in the quality of locally manufactured garments.

The government has announced plans to reopen the large mothballed Zambia-China Mulungushi Textiles factory in Kabwe before the end of 2012 to provide employment for youth workers.[6] The government holds a 36% stake in the company, with Qingdao Textiles owning the other 64%.

Competitiveness. Regional trade agreements through COMESA and the SADC that allow for duty-free importation of raw materials and finished garments make it difficult for Zambia to compete with other countries in the region because of its higher freight costs.

Challenges. The market price for cotton yarn is volatile and this is exacerbated by fluctuations in the ZMK/US$ exchange rate.

7.2 Sector Profile: Leather

There are five leather tanneries in Zambia, but only one—Zamleather—is currently operating at full capacity.

Two other companies are operational: Keembe Tanning Leather Works Limited, which subcontracts work from Zamleather, and Tata Tannery Limited, which bought the formerly government-owned tannery in Kabwe and processes wet blue there.

Zambia Bata Shoe Plc, which had been a leading Zambian shoe manufacturer, recently sold its shoe manufacturing machinery to Evambo, a company that makes pata-patas (flip-flops). Evambo has recruited a number of Bata's middle managers and is now making school shoes for sale to Bata. Bata's retail outlets sell mostly imported shoes, while it continues to manufacture gumboots.

Small-scale, informal and peripheral activities. There are a small number of cottage-industry outfits specializing in the high-end manufacture of leather handbags and similar items, mainly targeting tourists.

[6] Mulungushi Textiles to employ youths. *Zambia Daily Mail*, 1 July 2012.

TABLE 7.2. Leather and leather products export earnings, 2005–10 (all figures in thousands of US$).

2005	2006	2007	2008	2009	2010
3,959	4,854	5,829	10,143	7,368	4,809

Source: Exporter Audit Report 2010, Zambia Development Agency.

Supply and marketing chain. Two-thirds of leather comes from abattoirs such as Zambeef, with the remainder coming from small-scale suppliers.

Most hides are exported, with a small amount of value added making safety boots and workwear, usually for mining companies.

Export status and potential. The level of exports of leather and leather products is shown in Table 7.2.

It is illegal to export raw hides from Zambia, but of the official 210,000 cattle slaughtered annually, Zamleather tans only around 90,000. It is conjectured that many of the remaining hides are smuggled out of the country in their raw form via neighbouring countries to the Far East, or mixed with South African exports that fetch a higher price.

Policy context. Countries such as India are seen as providing more support to their national leather industry through help with effluent treatment and hide collection and through tax incentives. Zambian companies face a 15% import duty on shoe components such as toecaps, eyelets and heels.

The government has considered following the Ethiopian model, which restricts exports of leather to which value has not been added. This move would not be welcomed by the industry.

The ZABS lacks capacity and its certification is not currently internationally recognized. This is one reason for the lack of orders from mining companies.

ISO certification involves substantial costs for firms, and there is lack of local capacity for testing.

Competitiveness. There is an insufficient supply of high-quality hides for the sector to achieve economies of scale and operate profitably.

While Zamleather is able to secure high-quality hides from its parent company, Zambeef, it has still seen its average hide size drop from 2.8 square metres to 2.6 square metres in recent years. In order to use low-grade hides it has turned to the manufacture of shoes, boots and protective clothing. Other tanneries lack outlets for low-grade wet blue, and the cost of freight makes it uneconomic to export to Pakistan and India, where it is in demand to make shoes.

The requirement to pay immediately for raw hides, chemicals and freight, coupled with payment terms of 60 days on wet blue, add to firms' cash flow difficulties.

Challenges. Zambian leather is generally considered to be of relatively low quality, and prices reflect this.

There is a lack of support for the industry from the government and other potentially large customers such as the mining industry, who prefer to buy imported finished leather goods.

Illegal export of raw hides and low-quality hides are key problems facing the sector.

Poor quality could be addressed

- by enforcing existing legislation on branding standards and disease control (poor branding practices damage hides, as does skin disease); and
- by improving the quality of machinery in smaller abattoirs, where poor cutting of hides from carcasses causes damage to the hides.

The industry as a whole faces a shortage of skilled Zambian chemists and shoemakers as existing qualified employees reach retirement age and as work permits for expatriate staff become harder to obtain. The recruitment of skilled younger entrants is limited by a lack of educated applicants in some regions, and by competition from other industries for educated staff.

Sales of imported second-hand salaula shoes are also a threat to the sector.

7.3 Profiles of Major Firms

7.3.1 Unity Garments Limited

Basic details. Unity Garments is part of the Unity group of companies based in Ndola, and it is the largest garment manufacturer in Zambia, with an annual turnover of US$2m, of which some US$600,000 is from exports. It had 120 employees in May 2012. Group turnover is approximately US$40 million.

History. The Unity group was founded by Manu Shah, a Zambian citizen of Indian origin who came to Zambia in 1953.

He began trading locally in basic commodities such as salt and sugar in 1965, setting up a shop with his uncle and a local partner to supply basic commodities to plantation workers. He diversified his business interests throughout the 1970s and 1980s, encompassing investments in insurance, farming and manufacturing, and became a leading figure in the Indian business community.

Since then the Unity group has grown to incorporate three divisions—Unity Garments, Unity Packages and Unity Distributors—as well as the original trading company (Tops Trading Company).

The Shah family was originally a silent partner in the Unity Garments factory but acquired it outright when its British-Indian partners emigrated in 1972.

Current activities and products. Unity Garments originally supplied casual wear and trousers to parastals and retail stores, with the mining sector not being a major outlet. As a result, the company was able to withstand the mining sector collapse in 1983/84 that affected many of its competitors.

The more recent resurgence in the mining sector has resulted in an increase in demand for workwear, and there has also been a more general rise in demand for specialized and technical workwear and uniforms, as opposed to basic overalls, dustcoats and work suits, as a result of more government inspections of factories. Unity Garments has grown by identifying these niches and providing faster lead times than importers, and by being better able to accommodate variations in sizes.

Organization and management. Manu Shah remains chairman of the group, while his son Kam Shah is managing director.

Three professional managers—of Indian and Zambian origin—run the group's three divisions.

Firm capabilities. Unity Garments has the capacity to make 10,000–12,000 garments per month and was operating at around 60% capacity in mid 2012.

Supply and marketing chain. Unity Garments formerly imported fabric from South Africa and Zimbabwe but it now sources mainly from China, Taiwan and Kenya, with small amounts of fabric coming from India and Pakistan.

The company has workwear supply contracts with mining companies in Zambia and the Democratic Republic of the Congo, including the large Mopani and Kansanshi mines as well as smaller mines (including some Chinese-owned operations), and with National Milling and National Breweries.

Exports. Around 30% of the production of Unity Garments is exported, mainly to the Democratic Republic of the Congo. The company has also recently been supplying school trousers to Zimbabwe. Export earnings were around US$600,000 in 2011.

Until recently the firm also exported hospital uniforms to the US under the African Growth and Opportunity Act. It has a manufacturing-under-bond facility. The company has implemented the Worldwide Responsible Apparel Production certification programme.

Recent developments. Unity Garments hopes to increase its workforce from 120 to around 250 during 2012.

It is planning to relocate to a larger neighbouring new factory with an additional 300 sewing machines. Turnover of US$3 million is targeted for 2012.

Development agenda. The group is diversifying into residential and commercial property development. It is also planning to start a limestone mining operation.

7.3.2 Zamleather

Basic details. Zamleather, a subsidary of Zambeef (see full profile in Chapter 4), is Zambia's leading tannery. Its turnover was around US$2.5 million for the year to 30 September 2011. It employs 160 staff, of which 95 are factory workers.

History. Zamleather was established in 1997 when Zambeef took over the tannery business of Asaria Leather, to which it had been selling its hides, after it became dissatisfied with payment flows. It contributes around 1% of Zambeef's gross turnover and profit.

Current activities and products. Zamleather's Lusaka tannery processes all of Zambeef's cattle hides—around 5,000 per month—plus an additional 2,500 or so from third-party suppliers. Its highest-quality output is exported as wet blue, while the remainder is made into safety, security and military boots, school shoes and protective clothing. It produces around 300 pairs of shoes per day, which it sells under its Zamshu brand.

Organization and management. The company is run by a professional general manager who reports to the Zambeef senior management.

Skilled leather technologists oversee wet blue and finished leather production, and a trained and experienced shoe production manager oversees the production of shoes and personal protective equipment. Part of the shoe and personal protective equipment stitching is subcontracted to a small number of individual specialists.

Firm capabilities. Zamleather is operating at full capacity, working night shifts and overtime to meet demand. The company believes it could sell substantially greater volumes if its capacity were extended.

Supply and marketing chain. While two-thirds of Zamleather's hides come from its Zambeef parent, the remainder are bought from small-scale suppliers who are often unreliable.

Safety boots are made for the Mopani mine and for Konkola Copper Mines Plc, security boots are sold to private security companies, and school shoes are sold to Zambian outlets of the South African-based PEP Stores and direct to the public. A small quantity of military boots is supplied to the Zambia Air Force, but government orders are quite small overall.

Exports. Some 60% of output is exported as wet blue hides. The value of exports fluctuates with world market price: it can range from US$700,000 to US$1.5 million per annum.

Development agenda. Zamleather is considering expanding its capacity by adding additional machines and production lines.

Zamleather wishes to reduce the share of its output that is exported as wet blue from 60% to 25% by adding value to the remainder. Its target is to export its highest-quality output to the automotive market in Europe or South Africa, which demands very high quality and pays higher prices.

Chapter 8

WOOD PRODUCTS

8.1 Sector Profile

Background and overview. Zambia's commercial timber plantations consist mostly of soft pine and eucalyptus, with a total standing volume of more than 8 million cubic metres, located in the Copperbelt and South-Western provinces of the country. Pine is used in furniture manufacturing and in the construction industry, and gum poles are processed for the mining industry. The exotic plantations of pine and eucalyptus are managed by the privatized Zambia Forest and Forestry Industries Corporation (ZAFFICO), whose primary business is to regenerate the exotic species and sell mature trees to sawmills.

There are also a number of hardwood species such as *Brachystesia Boehmi* (Musamba), *Angolensis* (Mukwa) and *Petrocarpus Angolesis* (Mubanga). Most of the logging activities for natural indigenous forest take place in the Western, Southern, Eastern and North-Western provinces. The products that are manufactured and exported include particle board, railway sleepers, softwood and hardwood sawn timber, treated transmission poles, doors and frames, parquet tiles and edge-glued panels (Figure 8.1).

Exports of wood products have increased steadily despite challenges such as dwindling stockfeed and despite a growing domestic market, particularly from the construction industry. This increase in exports reflects significant investment in more efficient and diversified machinery (Table 8.1).

Profiles and lines of business of large firms. Bisonite Zambia Ltd (formerly PG Bisonite) and Wood Processing Industries Ltd are the two main firms engaged in the manufacture of wood products such as particle board, sawn timber, timber mouldings and surface-upgraded particle board. Bisonite Zambia is profiled in the next section.

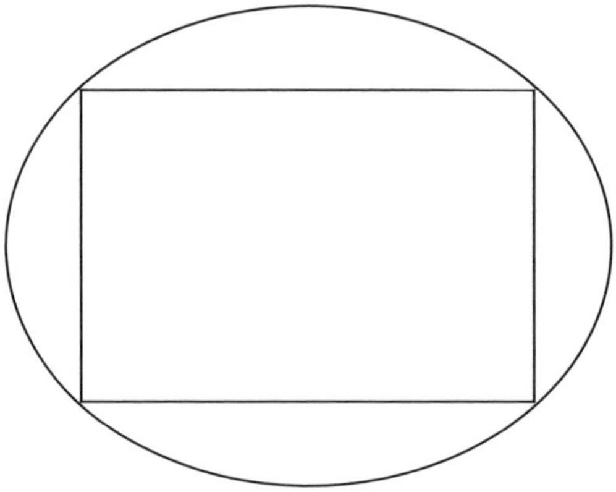

FIGURE 8.1. Particle board production. The cross-section of a log: the inner rectangle represents the section cut for sale as sawn timber; the outer discarded areas are those saved for conversion to particle board.

TABLE 8.1. Wood products export earnings, 2005–10 (all figures in thousands of US$).

2005	2006	2007	2008	2009	2010
3,468	4,503	5,017	14,762	7,340	12,761

Source: Exporter Audit Report 2010, Zambia Development Agency.

Wood Processing Industries is owned by a local Indian family who have been in the business for more than 30 years, and the firm accounts for 60% of total domestic sales (with Bisonite Zambia accounting for the remaining 40%). Wood Processing Industries has well-established distribution channels but produces only 2.5 m board, as opposed to Bisonite Zambia's 7 m board.

Profiles and lines of business of medium-sized firms. Copperbelt Forestry Company Limited was incorporated in 2000 after taking over ZAFFICO's Kafubu and Kalibu sawmills and joinery and wood-preservation assets. It employs an estimated 100 people.

Copperbelt Forestry Company is the main supplier of transmission poles to the national power supplier, Zambia Electricity Supply Corporation (ZESCO).

Small-scale, informal and peripheral activities. Small-scale saw millers make up an estimated 60% of the untreated wet timber market. However, their recovery rates are very low, and with the domestic market becoming more sensitive to quality, small-scale players are now under pressure to invest in better integrated production and enhanced skills.

Supply and marketing chain. Round wood is sourced from ZAFFICO, resin (urea-formaldehyde) is imported from South Africa, and light phenous oil for firing-up is sourced from the local Indeni oil refinery.

Export status and potential. The main export markets for wood and wood products are in South Africa, Zimbabwe, Botswana, Tanzania, Malawi, Namibia, Europe and the US.

Policy context. A UN Food and Agriculture Organisation assessment in 2010 reported that almost two-thirds of Zambia is forested, but deforestation is estimated to have depleted resources at the rate of 0.32% per year between 1990 and 2010. Forests cover 50 million hectares, with plantations making up around 62,000 hectares.

The rising demand for timber in Zambia has led to government-owned ZAFFICO earmarking US$95,000 for a feasibility study to assess more than 70,000 hectares of land for forestry plantations in Luapula, Muchinga and Northern provinces. The ZAFFICO plantation in Ndola covers 48,000 hectares and employs 2,000 seasonal employees, with timber production expected to increase in the future. The private sector has been urged to take part in regeneration schemes.

Challenges. ZAFFICO is the sole supplier of exotic softwood in the country and it sets the price.

8.2 Profile of a Major Firm

8.2.1 Bisonite Zambia Ltd

Basic details. Bisonite Zambia employs 78 permanent and 10 casual staff. Its turnover was US$1 million in 2009.

History. Bisonite Zambia (formerly PG Bisonite Ltd) was founded in 2003 by a consortium that came together to buy the assets of Sapco, a company founded by local Indian businessmen in 1999 as a manufacturer of chipboard and particle board. The consortium included PG Industries of Zimbabwe along with Zambian businessmen, but the majority shareholder is the Public Service Pension Fund (PSPF), holding 96% of the business.

Bisonite Zambia began commercial operations in 2004, and the company was recapitalized, with the PSPF investing in machinery and technology. A strategic partner is currently being sought.

Current activities and products. Bisonite Zambia makes particle board, sawn timber, timber mouldings and surface-upgraded particle board. It also produces other timber products including raw board and kiln-dried board as well as value-added skirting board, picture and window frames, and mining housing units. Kiln-dried timber is exported to Namibia.

Organization and management. The managing director, Francis Pindani Nyirenda, and senior management are seconded from the PSPF to manage operations. Staff are trained locally, though technical expertise and skills are occasionally sought from Zimbabwe.

Firm capabilities. The plant runs at 83% of nameplate capacity, processing 60 cubes of timber per day.

Bisonite Zambia is the only company in the country that produces 7 m long particle board.

Supply and marketing chain. Timber is sourced from ZAFFICO, the sole supplier of exotic softwood in the country.

Resin (urea-formaldehyde) is imported from South Africa as there are no provisions for local supply—the limited market for the product makes future supply locally unlikely. Machinery, including hydraulic press pumps for the particle board line, couplets and moulding machines, and spare parts are imported mostly from Germany and occasionally from South Africa. Light phenous oil for firing-up is sourced from the local Indeni oil refinery.

Wholesale supply in Zambia is distributed to warehouses in Chipata, Lusaka, Ndola and Solwezi. There are also three main distribution points in Zimbabwe, in Harare, Bulawayo and Masvingo.

Exports. Fifty percent of Bisonite Zambia's products are exported, to Zimbabwe, Namibia and Tanazania. The firm's product quality, competitive pricing and production of 7 m long particle board, as well as short board, give it an advantage over other exporters.

One factor that holds back expansion in the export market is the inability of wholesalers to pay on delivery.

Recent developments. Bisonite Zambia is in the process of reaching an agreement with ZAFFICO to source waste wood material that can be used in the production of particle board. The company has already invested significantly in efficient machinery to reduce losses from human error and to decrease waste. It is currently looking for further investment to establish a self-sufficient supply of softwood, in particular eucalyptus, which is faster growing than pine but has similar qualities. It is also exploring new export opportunities in Malawi.

Chapter 9

PAPER AND PACKAGING

9.1 Sector Profile

Background and overview. Most packaging materials used by manufacturing companies in Zambia are imported from South Africa, China, India and Europe. The domestic industry produces a range of products including tissue paper, paper serviettes, exercise books, polythene products and PET packaging (Table 9.1).

Profiles and lines of business of large firms.

Sobi Industries is a local leader in the manufacture of tissue paper and school exercise books. It is profiled in the next section.

Nampak Zambia Limited is Zambia's largest packaging company, and its sole manufacturer of conical cartons, which are used for (opaque) beer. It is profiled in the next section.

Capellaro Investments Ltd, another large packaging company, operates the former parastatal business of Kabwe Industrial Fabrics Limited. It makes polypropylene and polyethylene bags, plastic sheets and twine. It is profiled in Chapter 15.

Polythene Products Zambia Limited is a large producer of plastic bags.

Unity Packages Limited, part of the Tops group of companies, is Zambia's largest corrugated converter, making cardboard boxes, with an estimated market share of 65%. It recently invested US$7 million in its factory and machinery. Its turnover is US$12 million, with around 10% of its products exported to the Democratic Republic of the Congo and Zimbabwe. It has 70 employees and aims to increase that number to 120.

Established in February 1993, the company manufactures various corrugated paper board products for sale to large- and small-scale packaging users in Zambia and for export to the Democratic Republic of the Congo. The company has invested in delivery vehicles, computerization and waste

TABLE 9.1. Contribution to GDP of paper and paper products at current prices (all figures in millions of US$).

2000	8
2001	11
2002	13
2003	18
2004	24
2005	31
2006	37
2007	43
2008	65
2009	82
2010	113
2011	148

Source: The Monthly (May 2012), Central Statistical Office.

management systems. It sources its machinery from the Far East; this includes two graphics printers, which enable it to undertake four-colour printing, and the equipment needed to cut dies. The changes it has made to keep pace with changing technology have been important in attracting new customers.

The company manufactures 600–700 mt of packages per month and has the capacity to produce 1,000 mt. It maintains large on-site stocks of paper and raw materials such as inks, adhesives and essential spares.

It supplies packaging for biscuits, cosmetics, detergents, drinks, explosives and sweets, and for the yarn industry. It is also an approved box maker for fruit, flowers, meat and vegetables, and it also makes takeaway boxes for fast food.

Small-scale, informal and peripheral activities. There is a large and growing informal sector among street vendors and small-scale distributors trading packaging products, and this informal market is thought to supply much of its output to the Democratic Republic of the Congo.

Supply and marketing chain. Packaging is mostly sourced from South Africa, with carton board coming from Sweden and Finland. Recycled paper and print paper is imported from Sweden, South Korea, South Africa, Egypt and other countries in the SADC region; it is used in the manufacture of folding cartons for detergents. Recycled paper is more competitively priced, but new paper is also purchased from abroad as it is not available locally. This is particularly so for print paper used in making school exercise books. Machinery, including printing presses, cutting and stitching technology, is imported from Europe. Wholesale distribution is through local contracts to major supermarkets.

Export status and potential. Nampak's exports are small but growing, shadowing the expansion plans of its main customer, SAB Miller's National Breweries opaque beer business in Ghana, Mozambique, Nigeria, Tanzania, Uganda and Zimbabwe.

Invesco Ltd and Sobi Industries also export a small proportion of their products, between 5% and 10% of total production, mostly through the informal sector. However, the scale of the informal sector is difficult to calculate. It is estimated that a large proportion of products are purchased by small-scale vendors in Zambia and then sold to small-scale operations abroad, particularly in the Democratic Republic of the Congo. Larger, more-formal traders include wholesale distributors who purchase stock from factories and warehouses in the Copperbelt and then transport it across to the Democratic Republic of the Congo. Transport logistics and the fact that there is no formal banking system in the Democratic Republic of the Congo makes selling directly to that country impractical.

9.2 Profiles of Major Firms

9.2.1 Sobi Industries Ltd

Basic details. Sobi Industries produces a wide range of paper and packaging products. It employs about 240 staff.

History. The company was founded by Soyeb Gheewala, the father of the current managing director, in 1972. Initially, the business sold paper bags, and from there it diversified into making toilet tissue paper. When the Zambian economy was liberalized, and as the cost of sourcing paper began to rise, Soyeb's father saw the opportunity to diversify and expand the business. He bought printing technology to make school exercise books and stationery materials and a group of companies—including Plastex Packaging, Amigo Foods, California Beverages and Marydale Farm—was established in a bid to diversify income. Each company is independent, with separate factories, but the group has a single head office in Lusaka's industrial area.

Plastex Packaging was established because paper became relatively expensive as a packaging option. It was one of the first companies in Zambia to make packaging from PET and it provides packaging materials for other companies in the group.

California Beverages Ltd is a beverages company producing local drinks, including the popular Apple Max and Just Juice. Packaging is sourced from Plastex Packaging. (The company is described in Chapter 5.)

Amigo Foods Ltd produces snacks for the local market and is the only manufacturer of potato crisps in the country. Ingredients are sourced from Marydale Farm.

Marydale Farm has a beef herd and cultivates wheat, maize, soya and potatoes. The maize and potatoes are used as the main ingredients for Amigo Food's snacks and crisps.

Current activities and products. Sobi Industries produces paper bags, exercise books, tissue products, paper serviettes and stationery.

Organization and management. The business is family run, with Mr Gheewala and his brother acting as joint managing directors for the whole group. Each company has a financial controller, a marketing manager and a purchasing department.

Firm capabilities. The company produces 5,000 mt of finished paper and tissue product annually.

Supply and marketing chain. Recycled paper and print paper are imported from Europe, South Africa, Egypt and other countries in the SADC region.

Wholesale distribution is through local contracts to major supermarkets including Spar, Pick n Pay and Shoprite. The company also participates in government tenders for local supply.

Sobi Industries has a market share of 60% in tissue paper and 50% in school exercise books.

Exports. Exports are minimal, accounting for about 5% of total sales to the formal sector. Freight costs are a major barrier for the export business. A high proportion of total sales in Zambia are made to small-scale buyers who come from abroad, particularly from the Democratic Republic of the Congo.

Recent developments. Sobi Industries is currently doing a feasibility study to maximize self-sufficient supply, i.e. sourcing its inputs from within the group. While importing waste paper is currently cost effective, producing paper locally could lower costs in the long term.

9.2.2 Nampak Zambia Limited

Basic details. Nampak Zambia produces packaging materials and is a wholly owned subsidiary of Nampak Ltd, the largest packaging company in the southern hemisphere and the most diversified packaging company in the world. The firm is Zambia's largest packaging company and its sole manufacturer of conical cartons. It has 200 employees.

History. Nampak Zambia's business is the result of a 2004 merger of Lusaka-based International Cartons & Packaging Ltd, Ndola-based Crown Cork Company Ltd and conical carton manufacturer Nampak Zambia.

Crown Cork Company was a subsidiary of the US-based Crown Cork & Seal Company Inc, which was formed in the late 1950s and began operations in 1964/65.

Crown Cork Company was sold to Nampak Ltd in 2004, following anti-trust clearance, as part of a wider 2002 sale of Crown Cork & Seal's Central and East African packaging interests to Nampak Ltd.

International Cartons & Packaging was originally a joint venture between Nampak Ltd of South Africa and Rothmans of Pall Mall Zambia (now British American Tobacco Zambia PLC).

International Cartons & Packaging had formerly supplied cup wrappers, seals and corrugated packaging for the cigarette industry, but following the formation of Nampak Zambia Ltd in 2002, the Lusaka factory began making conical cartons for opaque beer.

The company is now 100% owned by Nampak Ltd, which is listed on the Johannesburg Stock Exchange, through the Nampak Southern Africa Holding Company of Mauritius.

Current activities and products. The firm makes folding cartons for fast-moving consumer goods, conical cartons for opaque beer, labels and self-opening bags, HDPE plastic blow-molded and injection-moulded bottles, and snap-cap closures. Conical cartons account for 60–65% of the company's business, and it is the largest producer of such products in the Nampak group.

At its Ndola plant it makes metal bottle crowns for beer and carbonated soft drinks. It also produces cans for oil and paint, and steel drums for oil and for cobalt exports. It also has an 800 mt injection-moulding line for the manufacture of HDPE plastic crates, primarily for the beer and beverages industries.

Organization and management. The company is headed by a managing director, who is supported by two directors who are in charge of operations and finance. There are also production managers at both plants.

Firm capabilities. The company produces more than 300 million conical cartons per year, about 900 mt of board per month, around 32 million self-opening paper bags for sugar per annum, around 15 million units per annum of HDPE bottles and closures, 550–600 million bottle tops per annum, 60,000 steel drums per annum, and 400,000 crates per annum.

Supply and marketing chain. The firm sources plastic from South Africa and carton board from Sweden and Finland. It buys metal, for use in the manufacture of crown closures, from China, Germany and South Africa.

The company imports paper from Sweden and South Korea for the manufacture of folding cartons used for detergents.

The company's main customers include National Breweries and Midland Breweries (for conical cartons and plastic crates), Zambian Breweries (for crown closures and plastic crates), Parmalat (for HDPE milk bottles and tops), Zambia Sugar (for self-opening paper bags) and oil companies, Chambeshi Metals and Mopani Copper Mines for steel drums.

Exports. Nampak's exports are small but growing, shadowing the expansion plans of its main customer, SAB Miller's National Breweries. This reflects the brewer's growing sales of opaque beer in Ghana, Mozambique, Nigeria, Tanzania, Uganda and Zimbabwe.

Recent developments. The firm has recently expanded its product line and has begun to manufacture PET jars.

Development agenda. In the short term the firm hopes to enhance its high-tech, value-added plastic manufacturing business, moving away from simple packaging where market entry is relatively easy. This involves a greater focus on plastic closures for carbonated soft drinks, PET preforms and conical cartons.

It also intends to expand its international sales, mainly to the north of Africa.

Chapter 10

CONSTRUCTION

10.1 Sector Profile

Background and overview. The construction industry is one of the fastest-growing sectors in Zambia. It accounted for 12–15% of GDP between 2007 and 2011 according to the National Construction Council. The sector has continued to grow rapidly due to continued strong demand for residential, commercial and public infrastructure projects across the country.

Between 2004 and 2007 the real year-on-year growth rates averaged 19%, but the sector's growth rate fell in 2008 to 8.7% following cement and building materials shortages. In 2009 it was adversely affected by the effects of the global financial crisis on the country's construction activities (Table 10.1).

Despite these setbacks in 2008 and 2009, the sector has performed well since then, driven to a large extent by construction of commercial and residential buildings and the establishment of new mines. The sector recorded growth of 10% in 2010.[1]

The industry is one of Zambia's largest employers: it is estimated that between 13,000 and 15,000 people currently work in the sector.

The Ministry of Works and Supply is responsible for building and construction industry policy. It also promotes quality construction and maintenance of public infrastructure, and procures and manages government property.

The main statutory bodies in the construction industry are the Zambia Institute of Architects, the Engineering Institution of Zambia, the Surveyors Institution of Zambia, the National Council for Construction (NCC), and the Road Development Agency.

Government contracts for housing, roads and other projects are allocated through a bidding process that is advertised in the press.

[1] Directory Publishers of Zambia Ltd. 2011/12. *Zambia Review*, 12th edn.

TABLE 10.1. Annual real growth rates in construction, 2004–10.

Year	Growth rate (%)
2004	20.5
2005	21.2
2006	14.4
2007	20
2008	8.7
2009	9.5
2010	8.1

Structure of the industry. The activities of Zambia's major construction companies can be classified as follows.

- Heavy construction: civil projects, roads, infrastructure, industrial building, sewer systems and railways.
- Commercial building: public schools, offices, retail, hotels and public buildings.
- Residential building: houses, flats and villas.
- Communication: telecommunication systems, power transmission lines and related physical infrastructure.
- Energy: power stations, renewable energy and related physical infrastructure.

Supply and marketing chain. Foreign construction companies remain leaders in the industry. They are large, have technical expertise and modern equipment and are able to carry out large projects (e.g. long-distance roads, bridges and commercial centres). Strong economic growth domestically has increased demand for housing and business accommodation. Current estimates show that Zambia has a deficit in housing units of 2,000,000 units; this presents an opportunity for foreign firms.

Local firms tend to be small and medium sized. They are mainly involved in the rehabilitation of feeder and trunk roads in rural and urban areas.

Policy context. The construction industry is regulated by the NCC, an arm of the government. All member companies are registered, certified and licensed by the NCC.

The government promotes public–private partnership arrangements in the construction sector. China and India have both invested in large-scale projects of this kind.

The regulatory bodies the NCC, the Zambia Institute of Architects, the Engineering Institution of Zambia and the Surveyors Institution of Zambia

TABLE 10.2. The number of registered contractors in Zambia.

Category	Number of constructors	Grade 1	2	3	4	5	6
Building and housing	1,681	35	31	44	133	356	1,082
Civil works	220	30	5	24	30	56	72
Mining	195	11	1	4	19	33	127
Electrical and telecommunications	83	9	6	6	18	15	29
Roads	542	34	16	23	59	152	262
Specialists	10	1	—	1	—	2	6
Total	2,731	120	59	102	259	614	1,578

Source: National Construction Council Annual Report 2010.

strive to provide a level playing field for local and foreign professionals and firms. The local industry is at a disadvantage due to its lack of modern equipment. Access to finance remains a challenge for local contractors.

Contractor classification. The NCC classifies constructors by grade and is responsible for registering, monitoring and regulating all construction activities. The classification is based on the contractors' financial standing, managerial expertise, technical ability, logistical capacities and stock of equipment.

The contractors are graded from 1 to 6. Grades 1–3 are the highest gradings; companies with these grades can bid for large projects. Smaller companies are given grades 4–6. Contracts of about US$4 million and above are restricted to grade 1 companies. Contracts of between US$1.8 million and US$4 million are also open to grade 2 and 3 companies. Contracts worth less than US$1.8 million are open to companies with grades of 4–6.

The number of contractors has been growing since 2005 according to the NCC.[2] There are now 2,731 registered contractors in the industry. Table 10.2 describes registered contractors by category.

There are currently 14 registered quantity surveying consulting firms and 30 registered individual quantity surveyors,

Some 80 suppliers and manufacturers of construction materials and equipment were registered as of December 2009.

[2] National Construction Council. 2010. *National Construction Council Annual Report 2010.*

Challenges. Construction is experiencing the effects of globalization. It has seen an influx of contractors and consultants and this has created strong competition for local players.

Complexities in the terms of contracts are a common source of disputes and often lead to delays in meeting project objectives, while lack of competence, experience and coordination by consultants in the sector can lead to poor standards of work.

Local contractors have limited capacity in terms of logistics, equipment and finance and therefore find it difficult to carry out large-scale construction projects.

The average length of time taken to obtain a construction permit is 254 days, and the process involves 17 stages.

Poor supervision stands out as a major challenge on over 80% of projects executed by local contractors according to the NCC, while late payment on government contracts affects cash flow.

Construction equipment is available for purchase and for hire but banks impose stringent requirements to obtain loans, and a lack of financing mechanisms constitutes a serious obstacle for small contractors in the sector.

A lack of adequately qualified staff has hampered the performance of small-scale contractors.

Competitiveness. Local professionals and firms have found themselves unable to compete with their foreign counterparts mainly because of a lack of capacity in skills and resources.

Profiles and lines of business of large firms. Three leading firms—Velos Enterprises Limited, Nemerit Enterprises Limited and Zambia Engineering and Contracting Company Limited—are profiled in the next section.

Velos Enterprises Limited has a workforce of 180 full-time employees and an annual turnover of US$3 million. It is profiled in the next section.

Nemerit Enterprises Limited was established in 1990 and its first project was completed in 1991. It is profiled in the next section.

Zambia Engineering and Contracting Company Limited employs 170 people and has an annual turnover of US$3 million. It is profiled in the next section.

Alongside these large domestic companies, several large-scale Chinese contractors have entered the Zambian market since 1990. These companies include the following.

Jiangxi Construction Engineering (Group) Corporation Limited, which set up its Zambian operation in 1990. It is profiled in the next section.

China Jiangxi Corporation for International Economic and Technical Cooperation was founded in 1983; it is a state-owned enterprise. Its focus is on overseas business, with projects in more than 50 countries, and it is heavily involved in aid projects financed by the Chinese government. The Zambian branch of the company was founded in 1988 and it was among the first Chinese companies to enter the Zambian market.

Its main areas of business include road construction projects, building construction projects and municipal public works projects. These include the following.

- Two road rehabilitation projects between Kaoma and Mongu in Western Province with a total contract value of US$47 million.
- A 90 km asphalt road in Northern Province, which is valued at US$45 million.
- A construction project worth US$22 million for the Munali Center of Excellence for special education needs at Munali High School.
- A rehabilitation project worth US$6 million for the Roma Township Park in Lusaka; this was due for completion at the end of 2012.

The Zambian arm of the company has 60 permanent Chinese employees (managers, engineers and interpreters) and 300 Chinese contract workers, who are mostly technical staff. It has a total of about 4,000 Zambian employees.

China Henan International Cooperation Group Ltd was founded in 1983; it is a parastatal enterprise under the jurisdiction of Henan Province. The company's main business operations cover international engineering projects, consulting services for international projects, international human resources cooperation and exchange, mining development, agriculture investment, and infrastructure projects in overseas countries with financial assistance from the Chinese government. The company maintains and operates regional offices in over 20 countries and regions across Asia, Africa and Europe. Its branch in Zambia was established in 1998. It was the first Chinese company to enter the road construction sector.

The company's annual turnover averages US$50–60 million. The number of people it employs depends on the number of ongoing projects it has; on average there are 10–20 Chinese employees and 150–200 Zambian employees for each project.

Background. In 1983 the People's Government of Henan Province established China Henan International Cooperation Group Ltd. The group's Zambian operation was established in 1998.

The company focuses on road construction projects, which involve building roads, water supply and sanitation, bridges and substations.

Its recent and current projects include the following.

- The road between Serenge and Mansa, the road between Lusaka and Chirundu, and the road around Landless Corner.
- A bridge at Chiawa crossing on the Kafue river.
- A water supply and sanitation project in four towns in Eastern Province. This was completed in 2012; it supplies safe potable water to 100,000 people.
- The Kitwe, Kalulushi and Chambeshi Water Supply Project, which is funded by the African Development Bank.

Small-scale, informal and peripheral activities. There are various small-scale and informal enterprises in Zambia that offer construction services. These range from artisanal bricklayers and small-scale jobbing building businesses to wealthier property developers who construct their own residential or commercial developments on land acquired for the purpose or already owned by family concerns. Subdivision of farmland on the outskirts of towns is increasingly common, with vendors either building structures for sale or rent, or selling bare plots for development by purchasers.

10.2 Profiles of Major Firms

10.2.1 Velos Enterprises Limited

Basic details. Velos Enterprises operates as an independent entity within the Union Gold group structure. It has a workforce of 180 full-time employees and an annual turnover of US$3 million.

History. Velos Enterprises was founded in 1978 by Dinos Frangeskides, a Cypriot national, as a one-man operation engaged in construction. The business was inherited by his children and it remains a family business run by three family members.

Current activities and products. The company constructs shopping malls and hotels. These include Arcades Shopping Malls, Shoprite Stores and all the Protea hotels in Zambia.

Organization and management. The company is run by three members of the family, all of them professional engineers. All three are directors and each takes responsibility for specific departments.

Firm capabilities. The firm is able to undertake construction projects of any size. It is a grade 1 firm in construction projects not including roads. The company has been in the construction business for 34 years and has established a reputation for quality. It had a wide knowledge of the construction market, giving it an advantage over other firms. A good knowledge of where to source materials locally and where to find the lowest prices has enhanced its strength.

Supply and marketing chain. Building materials such as cement, blocks, aggregates, doors and timber are sourced within Zambia. The company uses its own transport to move equipment to construction sites. The firm does not import any materials directly.

The firm sources its construction equipment from South Africa and the UK.

Recent developments. The firm is completing construction of a mining equipment factory in Lusaka for Japanese manufacturer Hitachi.

Development agenda. The firm aims to continue executing large-scale construction projects, and within a few years it intends to construct a shopping mall in Livingstone and to construct two hotels in Lusaka and Ndola.

10.2.2 Nemerit Enterprises Limited

Basic details. Nemerit Enterprises was established and registered in 1990 and its first construction project was completed in 1991. It is a private limited company that was started with an estimated initial capital investment of US$400,000. Based in Lusaka, it is engaged in construction, technical and management consultancy and property maintenance. It has 260 permanent workers and employs up to 470 people in total including casual workers at peak times. The company's annual turnover is about US$9 million.

History. Nemerit Enterprises was founded by Ian Thurai Ratnam, a Sri Lanka national who was based in Sri Lanka at the time the company was founded but who is now based in Zambia. It began as a small company set up under a Regional Investment Act that allowed the founder and his partners to raise capital. The firm grew by managing property developments on behalf of clients.

The firm has steadily grown since its inception and has widened its business to include building projects, construction, technical and management consultancy, property maintenance and building contracting.

Current activities and products. The firm specializes in construction and in the maintenance of residential and commercial properties. It focuses on preserving the long-term economic value of buildings through the provision of appropriate maintenance and repair services. It is also involved in property development and management services in commercial, retail and industrial properties.

Organization and management. Nemerit Enterprises has a five-person board of directors. The managing director, who is the sole owner of the company, takes charge of the everyday operations of the company and answers directly to the board, which he chairs. The management team comprises the managing director, the chief quantity surveyor, the administration manager, the finance manager and a district manager.

Firm capabilities. The company has a full complement of qualified professional and technical staff, six of whom are registered members of the Engineering Institution of Zambia. The company has its own workshop and transport facilities, running a fleet of more than 30 vehicles. It also has its own construction plant and uses its own equipment in all projects. The firm depends wholly on in-house senior staff and does not outsource.

Supply and marketing chain. The company formerly sourced trucks from outside but has now increased its own stock. It occasionally hires heavy loading equipment. The company has its own plant that includes front loaders, rollers, cranes, trucks and tipper trucks.

The firm sources blocks, cement and sand domestically. On a typical project, 50% of materials are sourced locally and 50% are imported from South Africa and Ukraine and from the SADC region.

Recent developments. Nemerit Enterprises has launched a fast-track service for corporate clients. This provides fast and efficient emergency maintenance services. The team responds to all queries within 24 hours.

Development agenda. The company plans to focus more on commercial building developments over the next five years. It intends to develop partnerships with government and the private sector in doing this. The firm also plans to become involved in the development of affordable housing.

10.2.3 *Zambia Engineering and Contracting Company Limited (ZECCO)*

Basic details. ZECCO is a Lusaka-based construction company. The company employs 170 people full time and has an annual turnover of US$3 million.

History. ZECCO was established in 1965 as a joint venture between the Zambian and Yugoslavian governments as a wide-ranging construction company to serve the needs of parastatals. It was originally 65% owned by the Zambian state investment vehicle ZIMCO and 35% owned by EnergoProjekt of Yugoslavia. ZECCO was privatized in 1995; EnergoProjekt, a holding company of the then Yugoslavian government, exercised its contractual rights as an existing shareholder and bought the Zambian government's share.

Current activities and products. The firm is engaged in constructing commercial buildings and making concrete blocks.

Organization and management. ZECCO has a local board of directors that reports to the parent company's head office in Belgrade; ZECCO is a wholly owned Belgrade firm.

Firm capabilities. The company's longevity in Zambia has helped it understand local market requirements.

It also has professional staff and adequate equipment.

Supply and marketing chain. The company sources blocks and pavers locally. Steel is imported from South Africa, China and India.

The company uses its own trucks except for bulk material, for which it hires external contractors.

Recent developments. The firm's recent contracts include a 104-unit housing scheme and four double-storey blocks.

Development agenda. Over the next ten years the firm intends to venture into road construction. It also plans to bid for projects in the hydropower sector.

10.2.4 *Jiangxi Construction Engineering (Group) Corporation Limited*

Basic details. Jiangxi Construction Engineering (Group) Corporation is a state-owned enterprise founded 60 years ago in China's Jiangxi Province. The corporation's predecessor was the Construction Engineering Bureau of Jiangxi Province, which was founded in 1952. Jiangxi Construction Engineering has 11 subsidiaries, two directly managed enterprises and a senior technical school. It has set up 12 general construction engineering companies, as well as overseas companies and joint venture companies. Its scope of activities includes building construction, groundwork and foundations, high-rise structures, municipal public engineering, highway engineering, water conservancy and irrigation works, electromechanical installations, metallurgical engineering, fire-fighting facilities, and steel structure engineering.

The company's Zambian operation was established in 1990 under the name Huagang Zambia Company; it was one of the first Chinese companies to enter the Zambian market. It has about 150 Chinese employees and about 1,500 Zambian employees. Its annual turnover is about US$60 million. Its assets include machinery and equipment valued at US$15 million and houses and land worth US$6 million.

History. Under China's arrangement for foreign aid to Africa, the Chinese government matched each province of China with an African country; Jiangxi Province was linked to Zambia. Initially, Jiangxi Construction Engineering was involved in building hospitals, schools and public facilities, fully paid for by the Chinese government. Later, Jiangxi found business opportunities in the construction sector and established its operations in Zambia through a partnership with a Hong Kong based partner.

Current activities and products. The company's current activities include the construction of civil buildings, civil engineering projects, the building of roads and earthworks and general electrical and telecommunications work.

Current housing construction projects include the expansion projects for Konkola Copper Mines. This is the company's main area of specialization: construction projects for major companies such as copper mines, steelworks and cement plants. Although these projects are usually technologically demanding and construction schedules are tight, the company has a record of completing projects on time.

Its current road projects include a 170 km road contract (from Mbala to Nakonde) worth US$170 million; this work commenced in October 2011. The original contractor for the project was China CAMCE Engineering Co. Ltd., an enterprise run by central government; the project was later subcontracted to Huagang Zambia Company.

Organization and management. The management team is primarily made up of Chinese nationals. It includes a general manager and three deputy managers. There are also professional managers in charge of operations, technology, planning, finance and human resources.

The parent company provides financial support and additional staff; it also gives letters of guarantee, but Huagang Zambia Company has to cover all the costs it incurs at market prices.

Firm capabilities. Jiangxi Construction Engineering is classed as a grade 1 contractor in all its areas of operation.

Supply and marketing chain. Sand and stone are sourced locally: the firm extracts and crushes rock from nearby mountains. Construction equipment is imported from China and South Africa.

Challenges. The firm's main competitors are other Chinese firms operating in Zambia. There are between 10 and 20 relevant competitors depending on the area of operation.

Recent developments. In the 20 years following its foundation in 1990, the Zambian business grew very slowly. However, after a reform of the parent company in 2008–9, its business both in China and Zambia has expanded rapidly. This, combined with Zambia's construction boom, has led to the company's recent growth.

Development agenda. The company is now preparing to bid for a substation project for a Chinese copper mine in Chambeshi and for a cement plant in Ndola. It is also considering investing in real estate.

Chapter 11

BUILDING MATERIALS

11.1 Sector Profile

Background and overview. Zambia's building materials sector has grown substantially over the past five years with the rise in the construction of housing and commercial developments. Construction and rehabilitation of infrastructure, including roads, schools, clinics, dams, shopping centers and irrigation schemes, have also driven demand and have created new employment opportunities for skilled artisans.[1]

The building materials industry produces a wide range of products including asbestos pipes, roofing sheets and tiles, and ceramics. Cement production is considered separately in Chapter 12. A high proportion of imported products are sourced from South Africa.

Building materials, including cement, accounted for some US$70 million of export earnings in 2010; this represented more than an eightfold increase since 2005 (Table 11.1) and was approximately 5% of the country's total non-traditional exports.

Supply and marketing chain. Basic materials such as building sand and stones are supplied by small local firms and entrepreneurs, and there is a growing industry in concrete block manufacture at artisan level, replacing the more traditional laterite-based bricks made in rural areas. Transport is either outsourced or provided by supplier firms for an additional charge.

Challenges. The high cost of mortgages and other loans and their lack of availability are serious constraints on the building of new residential property.

Export status and potential. The major export markets are the Democratic Republic of the Congo, Burundi, Malawi and South Africa. Other markets are Tanzania, Kenya, Mozambique and Zimbabwe, with cement accounting for the bulk of cross-border trade.

[1] Zambia Development Agency. 2012. *Directory of Zambian Exporters 2011.*

TABLE 11.1. Building materials export earnings, 2005–10 (all figures in thousands of US$).

	2005	2006	2007	2008	2009	2010
Building materials	8,446	14,351	7,911	35,684	24,377	70,234

Source: Exporter Audit Report 2010, Zambia Development Agency.

Profiles and lines of business of large and medium-sized firms. The building materials industry comprises a handful of large manufacturers, such as TAP Zambia Limited and Safintra Zambia Ltd, a number of medium-sized producers, and an artisan sector. In recent years, local firms have expanded and new companies have entered the market.

TAP Zambia Limited makes roofing sheets, tiles and related products. It is profiled in the next section.

Safintra Zambia Ltd produces metal roofing materials. It is profiled in the next section.

Aluworks Industries Limited is based in Lusaka and was established in 2009. It has a modern manufacturing plant that produces a range of roofing sheets in various gauges and colours; its roofing sheets are made from galvanized iron, aluminium and aluminium–zinc and are either of inverted box rib or corrugated design. The plant also has facilities for slitting flat sheets, bull nosing and manufacturing roofing ridges, gutters and flashings. The plant has a monthly production capacity in excess of 400,000 m of roofing sheets.

ClassEcon Roofing Africa Limited was incorporated in 2010 and is backed by a UK investment company. The company makes steel roofing sheets in various thicknesses, selling them in galvanized and prepainted form. It also makes roofing sheets from aluminium and stainless steel and supplies roofing accessories including ridges, valley gutters, flashings, rotating ventilators, insulation films, and fasteners.

Ductshop Zambia is based in Lusaka and makes duct systems for heating, ventilation and air-conditioning units.

Kavino Limited, which produces drawn wire and galvanized roofing sheet, is described in Chapter 13.

Small-scale, informal and peripheral activities. There are numerous small-scale firms and individuals moulding cement blocks, crushing stones and providing sand. They are largely unregulated.

11.2 Profiles of Major Firms

11.2.1 TAP Zambia Limited

Basic details. TAP Zambia makes endurite and Trafford brand tiles, roofing sheets, pipes and decorative garden ceramics from fibre cement (asbestos-cement). It has 150 permanent employees and up to 100 casual workers at peak times.

History. TAP Zambia was established in 1943 as a trading subsidiary of the UK firm Turner Asbestos Products (Turner and Newall). In 1955 it began manufacturing domestically. The company was acquired in 1996 by the African Resource Group, which operates in South Africa, Zimbabwe and Zambia.

Current activities and products. TAP Zambia produces roofing sheets, garden decor, flowerpots, pressure pipes for water reticulation, and sewer pipes.

Organization and management. The CEO, who reports to a board of directors and oversees operations, is assisted by a chief financial officer and a director of sales and marketing. The company is managed by African Resource Group.

Firm capabilities. The firm is ISO 9001:2000 certified. Its products are also certified by the South African Bureau of Standards.

Supply and marketing chain. The firm is located alongside the Lafarge cement plant in Chilanga, from which it sources cement. The other main input of TAP Zambia's roofing sheets, asbestos fibre, is sourced from AA Mines in Zimbabwe, which is owned by TAP Zambia's parent company (African Resource Group).

TAP Zambia uses local trucking companies for export sales; it hires these companies on behalf of its foreign customers.

Exports. The firm's exports, mainly of roofing sheets, constitute 10–15% of overall sales. Its main export destinations are the Democratic Republic of the Congo, Mozambique, Malawi and Kenya.

Competition. TAP Zambia's main competitor in roofing products is Harvey Products, which imports tiles from South Africa.

Recent developments. The company has recently begun to produce galvanized roofing sheets. It has set up a new division, TAP ZAM Construction, to handle construction services.

It has also set up a waste-management operation, TAP ZAM Waste Management Services, and an unplasticized polyvinyl chloride (uPVC) plant to produce pipes for water supply and sewer lines.

Development agenda. The firm now plans to enter the real estate market.

11.2.2 Safintra Zambia Ltd

Basic details. Safintra Zambia, which produces metal roofing materials, is part of the South Africa-based SAFAL group of companies. It employs 106 workers.

History. The SAFAL group obtained an investment licence from the Zambia Development Agency in February 2006 and began operations under the name Steelbase later that year. The company changed its name to Safintra Zambia Ltd in 2007 to bring it into line with the group brand continent-wide.

Since then it has expanded by building an additional manufacturing base in Kitwe, and it has imported additional equipment from Japan and Taiwan for manufacturing different types of roofing sheet.

Current activities and products. Safintra Zambia manufacturers a range of roofing sheets under its brand names Versatile and Zamtile.

It also manufactures box-shaped roof sheets, whch are popular with industrial construction, galvanized roofing sheets and aluminium zinc-coated sheets.

The firm takes advantage of SAFAL's technology and expertise to constantly expand and improve its product range.

Organization and management. Safintra Zambia has one director who is appointed by SAFAL (who is also responsible for SAFAL's operations in Malawi) together with a sales and marketing manager and a head of finance.

Supply and marketing chain. As a member of the SAFAL Group, Safintra Zambia maintains backwards and forwards linkages with other companies within the group—particularly Mabati Rolling Mills in Kenya and other steel rolling companies in South Africa—which supply it with coated coils. Safintra Zambia also buys some inputs from Zambian producers: iron bars, angle iron and square tubes.

The company has distribution centres in Lusaka and in Kitwe (to serve the northern part of the country). Safintra Zambia sells through local dealers across the country.

Exports. Safintra Zambia does not export products directly, though some of its customers come from the Democratic Republic of the Congo and Tanzania.

Recent developments. The company has recently acquired a truck for delivery of its Saflok 700 concealed roofing sheets that enables direct transfer of the sheets from the truck to a customer's roof. The firm is currently planning to introduce a new line of stone-coated roofing sheets.

Chapter 12

CEMENT AND QUARRYING

12.1 Sector Profile

Background and overview. Strong growth in the construction sector over the past few years has brought about an increase in demand for cement (Table 12.1). The contribution of the construction sector to Zambia's GDP rose from 7.5% in 2009 to 15.5% in 2010. The total output of cement for 2010 at 1,127,000 mt was 37.9% higher than the 817,000 mt produced in 2009. The mining industry has contributed significantly to this increase.[1]

Structure of the cement industry. Before market liberalization in the early 1990s the cement industry was monopolized by Chilanga Cement, then a state-owned company. In 2007 the company was privatized and sold to the French multinational Lafarge, becoming Lafarge Cement Zambia.

Zambia now has three large domestic cement producers, of which Lafarge is the largest. In the fourth quarter of 2010 Lafarge's production rose by 14.9% to just over 251,000 mt.

Scirocco Enterprises, which operates under the trade name Oriental Quarries, started business in 1981. Oriental Quarries, based in Lusaka, had an estimated production of 109,500 mt in 2010.

Zambezi Portland Cement Limited began production in 2009. The company is based in Ndola and has an estimated production capacity of 330,000 mt per annum.

Ndola Lime Company has commenced discussions with a number of undisclosed potential partners on a possible joint-venture cement plant in the Copperbelt.[2]

[1] O'Hanlon, J. 2010. Lafarge Cement Zambia. *Business Exellence Online*: www.bus-ex.com/article/lafarge-cement-zambia.

[2] Ndola Lime plans cement production venture, Zambia. *International Cement Review*, 17 May 2012.

TABLE 12.1. Cement demand by volume (mt).

2009	817,223
2010	1,126,728
2011	1,428,855

Source: Zambia Review, 12th edn, Directory Publishers of Zambia Ltd (2011/12); *Quarterly Financial and Statistical Report 2011*, Bank of Zambia.

In 2011 Dangote Industries of Nigeria was awarded a licence to build a US$500 million cement processing plant in Masaiti in the Copperbelt with an initial production capacity of 3,500 mt per day.[3]

Stone quarrying has grown by a third in recent years due to increased demand for sand and crushed stones from the construction and mining industries.

Profiles and lines of business of large firms. Zambia's cement industry is dominated by the formerly state-owned Lafarge Cement Zambia—now part of the France-based Lafarge Group, which is the world's largest producer of cement—with local companies Zambezi Portland Cement and Scirroco Enterprises (trading as Oriental Quarries) as relatively new entrants.

Apart from the three major cement firms, there are two medium-sized quarrying companies. Ital-Terrazzo Limited was formed in 1969 by the Ventriglia family, who later founded Zambezi Portland Cement. Uniturtle Industries Zambia Limited was established in Lusaka in 1985 and has gradually expanded its activities and product lines to cover paving and exterior tiles, agriculture and stockfeed lime, tombstones, funeral services, window blinds, awnings and sporting trophies.

Small-scale, informal and peripheral activities. There are numerous small and informal enterprises involved in the supply and distribution of cement. There are also individuals who supply stones and other basic materials to builders.

Cement dealers. Various small enterprises sell cement in small quantities at relatively high prices.

Stone crushers. These are individuals involved in quarrying and crushing stones for sale to building and construction companies. They are informal and unregulated.

[3] State issues licence to Dangote for $500 million project. Lusakatimes.com, 13 August 2012.

Sand suppliers. Many individuals, based on the outskirts of major cities, sell sand. They are generally unregulated and have open stands from which they fill trucks to order.

Supply and marketing chain. Limestone is quarried locally. Coal is generally imported from Zimbabwe.

Export status and potential. Some cement is exported to markets in the SADC: the Democratic Republic of the Congo, South Africa, Tanzania and Zimbabwe. All cement for export is packed in reinforced 50 kg bags and export is exclusive of value added tax.

Policy context. Environmental issues are becoming an increasing concern, with regulation needed to ensure that environmental damage, such as water and air pollution, is minimized.

A serious shortage of cement supply, which led to substantial price increases, led to the commissioning in 2008 of Lafarge's Chilanga 2 plant.

Concerns have been raised about labour exploitation and child labour in the informal stone crushing sector.

Challenges. Electricity outages resulting from ZESCO's undercapacity present a challenge to cement manufacturers.

Manufacturers also complain of high fuel costs for transport.

12.2 Profiles of Major Firms

12.2.1 Lafarge Cement Zambia Plc

Basic details. Lafarge Cement Zambia, Zambia's leading cement producer, is part of the French Lafarge Group, the world's largest manufacturer of cement, aggregates and concrete. It is listed on the Lusaka Stock Exchange.

Located on the outskirts of Lusaka, Lafarge Cement Zambia has 611 staff. Its annual turnover for 2011 was US$167 million, with exports of US$54 million.

History. The firm was founded in 1949 as Chilanga Cement by the Northern Rhodesian government and the Colonial Development Corporation, now the Commonwealth Development Corporation. Cement production commenced in 1951, and between 1956 and 1957 two additional kilns were added. The aim was to provide cement for the Kariba Dam, which was then under construction.

In 1969 the Ndola plant was commissioned, with a second kiln added there in 1974. The company was privatized in October 1994 and CDC became the majority shareholder.

Early in 2001 the CDC reorganized its cement operations in Southern Africa to form Pan African Cement, which owned shares in Chilanga Cement, in Mbeya Cement in Tanzania, and in Portland Cement in Malawi. In May 2001 Lafarge acquired Pan African Cement from the CDC. It also acquired a further 34% of Chilanga Cement through a compulsory offer to minority shareholders. This allowed Lafarge to acquire its present 84.5% stake.

In 2007 the firm changed its name to Lafarge Zambia. The inauguration of a new US$120 million plant inaugurated at Chilanga in 2008 ('Chilanga 2') has enabled the company to double capacity to 1,300,000 mt of cement per annum.

Current activities and products. Lafarge Cement Zambia manufactures and sells cement and has two operating facilities: the Chilanga plant on the outskirts of Lusaka, and Ndola in Ndola. The firm also owns 14% of Mbeya Cement Company Limited.

Its products include its flagship Mphamvu brand and Powerplus (used in heavy industrial construction projects). Its latest brand is SupaSet, for block manufacture.

Organization and management. The board comprises seven directors, including independent non-executive directors. The roles of chairman and CEO are separate. An executive management committee is responsible for implementing strategies and policies determined by the board.

Firm capabilities. Lafarge draws on technical expertise from its company in Lyon, France.

The new Chilanga 2 plant increased Lafarge's capacity from 650,000 mt to 1,230,000 mt per annum, of which the Ndola plant contributes around 450,000 mt.

Supply and marketing chain. The two main raw materials used by the plants are limestone and phyllite. The Ndola plant is a dry process plant with a capacity of 450,000 mt per annum, while the Chilanga plant is a wet process plant. Limestone, shale and sand are the main materials used and all are sourced locally. The firm sources coal from Zimbabwe and subcontracts its transport.

Lafarge has a 75% share of the cement market in Zambia, selling direct from its plant to wholesalers and large-scale producers. Lafarge enjoys direct relationships with major mining companies such as Vedanta, First Quantum Minerals, Equinox and Glencore.

Competition. Lafarge's main competitors are Zambezi Portland Cement, profiled below, and Oriental Quarries, which is a supplier of aggregate and has a cement capacity of 80,000 mt per annum. Ready-mix concrete is supplied both by Oriental Quarries and by Brunelli, who source cement from Lafarge.

Exports. Lafarge exported 35% of its output, valued at US$54 million, in 2011. The main export destinations are the Democratic Republic of the Congo and Burundi. Lafarge exported about 14,000 mt of cement a month to the Democratic Republic of the Congo alone in 2010.

Development agenda. The firm now plans to further develop its business in ready-mix concrete.

The firm also aims to develop its corporate social responsibility initiatives focused on health, education and the environment.

12.2.2 Scirocco Enterprises Limited (Trading as Oriental Quarries)

Basic details. Scirocco Enterprises operates under the trade name Oriental Quarries. It has a workforce of 800 permanent staff and is the second largest cement manufacturer in Zambia.

History. The company was established in 1981 as a small stone-crushing operation in Lusaka, using predominantly second-hand equipment. It started as a family business run by Moustafa Saadi, Murad Saadi and Ahmed Saadi, who are Zambian citizens of Lebanese origin. The company has expanded into cement, aggregates, precast concrete walls, concrete blocks and ready-mix concrete, and also provides construction, mining, road building and transport services.

Its plant begun production of its Amaka brand of Portland cement in 2005, with an initial production level of 100 mt per day; the production level has since increased to 300 mt per day. Its cement is sold in 25 kg bags or delivered in bulk to customers' silos.

Current activities and products. The company is engaged in quarrying, construction, mining and building. It produces ordinary Portland cement, crushed stone aggregate, concrete blocks and ready-mix concrete.

Organization and management. Oriental Quarries is managed by the three founding directors of the company together with a chairman of the board. They are supported by professional directors in key management positions.

Firm capabilities. Oriental Quarries was the first company to introduce ready-mix concrete to Zambia, and it continues to dominate that market. It is one of the largest producers of aggregates, concrete blocks and paving stones in the country.

Scirocco Enterprises has three aggregate crushing plants, with a combined output of more than 4,000 mt per day, producing quarry sand, chippings and concrete stones.

The firm operates its own fleet of trucks, including flatbed and tipper trucks with the ability to handle bulk cargo. The tippers have the capacity to deliver 2,000 mt of aggregate pre day in the Lusaka area. Oriental Quarries makes bulk deliveries of cement to large customers.

Supply and marketing chain. The firm's sand and stones come from its own quarry. Transport is available to customers for an extra charge.

Exports. The company's main market is domestic but it also exports to SADC member states, with Malawi, South Africa and Namibia as major destinations. Satellite tracking is used for all trucks for security and reliability.

Recent developments. The firm has commissioned a new 50,000 mt per day concrete block plant, a precast concrete panel factory, and a cement and concrete laboratory.

Development agenda. In the next few years the company hopes to launch a new 300 mt per hour crusher and a window factory to boost its business and meet increasing demand.

It also plans to move into construction.

12.2.3 Zambezi Portland Cement Limited (ZPC)

Basic details. ZPC began operations in 2009. It operates a plant in Ndola, which produces 330,000 mt of cement per year. The company employs about 600 workers.

History. The history of ZPC began in 1957, when the Ventriglia family from Italy settled in Zambia. In 1969 the family established a company, Ital-Terrazzo Ltd, in Ndola. The firm is well known throughout the country for its terrazzo flooring and roof tiles.

In 2004 Antonio Ventriglia and his son Daniele established a cement plant in Ndola. Despite a difficult economic climate, the family went on to expand their existing Ndola factory to establish ZPC.

Current activities and products. The firm produces 1,200 mt of cement per day.

Organization and management. The ownership and management of the company is the subject of current legal proceedings.

Supply and marketing chain. ZPC's own quarry supplies limestone. Gypsum and coal are also sourced locally.

Exports. The firm exports to the Democratic Republic of the Congo, Malawi, Burundi, Mozambique and Zimbabwe.

Development agenda. In April 2012 the company announced plans to expand its plant at a cost of US$70 million, boosting production to 1,500 mt of cement per day.[4]

In the next five years the firm intends to build another factory in the Chilanga area and plans to supply to a wider region of the country. The firm also hopes to build its own lime plant.

[4] Zambezi Portland to invest $70 million in expansion project. *Zambia Daily Mail*, 16 April 2012.

Chapter 13

METALS, ENGINEERING AND ASSEMBLY

13.1 Sector profile

Background and overview. Basic metals and fabricated engineering products accounted for 25% of total manufacturing GDP between 2000 and 2010.[1]

This chapter covers the manufacture of products from copper and steel. Copper products include copper wire, cable and rods, alloys and ingots, carbon brushes, switchgears, pipes and railway sleepers.[2] Steel products include deformed bar, flat bar and metal tubes. Building materials (window and door frames, roofing, etc.) are dealt with in Chapter 11.

Supply and marketing chain. Copper from the mining sector provides raw materials for many companies, including Metal Fabricators of Zambia PLC (ZAMEFA), which dominates export earnings in the sector. Steel mills, such as Universal Mining and Chemical Industries Limited, rely on buying scrap metal as their primary raw material (see Tables 13.1 and 13.2 and Figure 13.1).

Secondary manufacturers such as those making door and window frames and roofing sheets usually buy imported steel from South Africa (sold through local distributors), although the establishment of local steel mills such as Universal Mining and Chemical Industries Limited and Good Time Steel has provided a local alternative to imports.

Policy context. Despite the scale of Zambia's copper mining, the manufacture of copper products is limited, with cable and rod makers ZAMEFA and Kavino the only significant manufacturers. While the government has been keen to encourage more companies into the sector, there are serious challenges, as we note below.

[1] Zambia Association of Manufacturers. 2011. *Annual Report 2011.*
[2] Zambian Development Agency. 2011. *Directory of Zambian Exporters.*

TABLE 13.1. Contribution of fabricated metal products to GDP at current prices (all figures in millions of US$).

2000	4.32
2001	4.34
2002	3.97
2003	3.97
2004	5.23
2005	6.65
2006	10.12
2007	13.20
2008	12.31
2009	8.35
2010	13.75
2011	20.34

Source: The Monthly (May 2012), Central Statistical Office.

TABLE 13.2. Engineering products export earnings, 2005–10 (all figures in thousands of US$; nominal prices).

2005	2006	2007	2008	2009	2010
96,419	288,592	210,495	225,702	154,940	190,577

Source: Exporter Audit Report 2010, Zambia Development Agency.

Export status and potential. ZAMEFA dominates exports with the sale of copper cables and wire.

Key export markets for this sector include South Africa, Tanzania, Zimbabwe, Malawi, Botswana, Namibia and the Democratic Republic of the Congo, with secondary markets in Uganda, the Philippines, Switzerland, Hong Kong, India, Mauritius and Mozambique.[3]

Competitiveness. A UKAid/World Bank-supported report of 2011 concluded that the local availability of copper does not provide Zambia with any substantial comparative advantage in copper fabrication.[4] In an industry in which proximity to consumer markets is the key driver, domestic and regional demand for copper products would need to grow substantially before any sizable expansion in Zambia's copper fabrication industry would be commercially viable, and such market growth will take time.

[3] Zambia Development Agency (2011).

[4] UKAid/World Bank. 2011. What is the potential for more copper fabrication in Zambia? In *Jobs and Prosperity: Building Zambia's Competitiveness Program.*

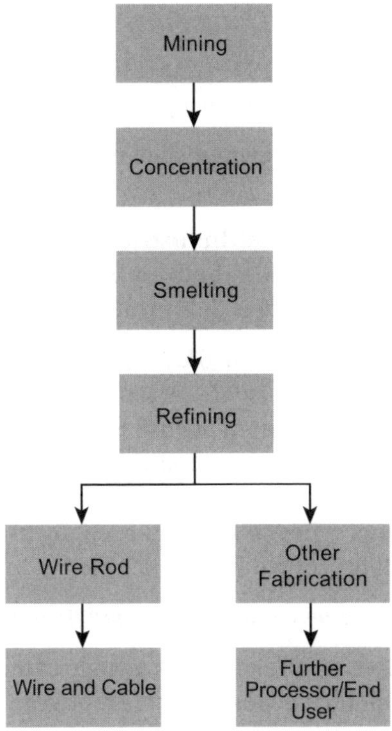

FIGURE 13.1. Copper industry value chain. *Source*: World Bank (2011).

Zambia has a poor reputation for quality in the steel sector, with buyers often preferring imports from South Africa or elsewhere over locally produced products. This is something that local manufacturers are aware of and are attempting to address.

Challenges. Further value addition to copper is constrained by a number of factors.

On the supply side, the price of copper is set by world markets, and proximity to the source of the raw material does not provide much advantage.

Copper fabrication requires some additional inputs (scrap and nickel for alloys) that are not produced in Zambia and are costly to import.

On the demand side, there is little domestic demand for copper products, and exporters face logistical difficulties and high freight costs.[5]

[5] UKAid/World Bank (2011).

Profiles and lines of business of large firms. There are four large firms.

Metal Fabricators of Zambia PLC (ZAMEFA) makes copper rods, cables and wires. It is profiled in the next section.

Good Time Steel is a Chinese-owned steel maker. It is profiled in the next section.

Universal Mining and Chemical Industries Limited is a recently established Zambian steel maker; it is now embarking on a venture that will mine iron ore for steel production. It is profiled in the next section.

Safintra Zambia Ltd belongs to the SAFAL group of companies. The group operates in Eastern and Southern Africa; it manufactures roofing products. The group obtained an investment license from the Zambia Development Agency in February 2006 and started operations as Steelbase Limited in the second half of 2006. It imported equipment from Japan and Taiwan for the manufacture of various types of roofing. It changed its name to Safintra Zambia Ltd in 2007. It is profiled in Chapter 11.

Profiles and lines of business of medium-sized firms.

Zamcapitol Enterprises in Lusaka makes a range of metal products including aluminium pots, metal toecaps for safety footwear, and gang nails (roofing truss plates) for strengthening wooden structures. It also manufactures water supply products and agricultural products. The company supplies toecaps to Zamleather and Bata. Gang nails are manufactured from both galvanized steel and mild steel and they are used in the reinforcement of transmission power pole ends and railway sleepers, as well as in the manufacture of wooden trusses. The firm's general engineering workshops offer a variety of services including milling, hydraulic pressing and lathe work. (It has a lathe with one of the longest beds in Zambia.) The company also manufactures its own steel multiplates, press work tools and machined and fabricated spares, and it carries out heat treatment services such as carburizing, annealing and tempering, and hardness testing.[6] The company employs 91 people.

Match Corporation manufactures ferroalloys. Its plant, which is situated in Luanshya, has a 3 MVA (MVA stands for the unit megavolt ampere) capacity open arc furnace for the production of ferrosilicon. It expects to begin production soon on a 6 MVA furnace for silico-manganese. It is not a fabricator.

[6] *Source*: www.thebestofzambia.com.

Scaw Limited manufactures high-chrome, low-chrome, forged grinding media balls, iron and steel castings, and deformed bars. It also produces industrial gases. It is profiled in Chapter 16.

Wire Force Zambia Limited makes brick force wire, diamond mesh wire, concrete reinforcing wire, barbed wire, tying wire and wire nails.

Morganite Zambia Limited produces electrical switchgears, motors and carbon brushes; it has 38 employees.

Meltcast Engineering Co. Ltd is a steel fabricator that makes water tanks, fuel tanks, and steel structures for mines. It employs 120 people.

Powerflex Zambia Limited makes industrial and mining spares. It carries out steel fabrication and erection and makes pipes, shafts, pins, bolts and nuts, flanges and locomotive wheels. It employs 150 people.

Non-Ferrous Metal Works (Zambia) Limited makes castings in bronze, brass, aluminium, copper, cast iron, steel and stainless steel. It employs around 56 workers.

Perway Industries Zambia Limited manufactures railway track fittings, nuts and bolts.

Saro Agro Industrial Limited manufactures trailers, hammer mills, water and fuel tanks. This is in addition to its main business of supplying machinery to the farming, mining and construction sectors. The company employs 240 people, of which 100 are engaged in manufacturing.

Afrope Zambia Limited makes aluminium wire, steel wire, screen mesh, scraper rope and wire rope slings. It employs 27 people.

Danyan Engineering has a metal engineering and fabrication workshop and also provides general engineering construction services for building construction, steel structure erection, machinery installation and repairs to equipment and engines.

Keren Motors Limited is a Zambian-owned company based in Lusaka. Since it was established in 1987 it has expanded from bulk haulage of dry cargo and petroleum products to metal fabrication, plant installation and general engineering services. Its core business is the manufacture and sale of bulk fuel tanks and underground storage tanks, but it can make up other metal items to order. Keren Motors originally developed its engineering workshops to fabricate tanks for their own fuel transporters, and to maintain their plant and equipment. The company also transports dry cargo, petroleum products and bulk mining material, supplies mining equipment and offers earth-moving and metal engineering services.[7]

Steel Tech Investment fabricates structural steel racks and industrial trailers. It also manufactures nuts and bolts and water tanks.

Small-scale, informal and peripheral activities. There are numerous small-scale engineering workshops making items to order. Informal artisan enterprises make window and door frames from mild steel sheet, and buckets, baths and other household utensils from galvanized mild steel sheet. These items are sold in markets and on the roadside.

13.2 Profiles of Major Firms

13.2.1 Metal Fabricators of Zambia PLC (ZAMEFA)

Basic details. ZAMEFA makes copper rods, cables and wires. Turnover in the year to 20 June 2012 was around US$220 million.

The labour force stood at 814 when the company was privatized in 1996.[8] Employment has dropped since and currently stands at around 300 employees, with staffing levels now being rebuilt following the global economic downturn.

History. ZAMEFA was championed by the first president of the Republic Dr Kenneth Kaunda, who wanted the country to have a company that produced copper products. ZAMEFA was founded in 1967 and officially opened in 1969; it was centrally located in the Copperbelt in Luanshya. It was 83% owned by government and 17% owned by Phelps Dodge (an American company with mineral prospecting rights throughout the Copperbelt) and Outokumpu Copper (a Finnish company that provided its casting machines).

ZAMEFA was privatized in 1996 and some 33% of the company was sold for US$3.2 million under preemption rights to Phelps Dodge, Outokumpu Copper and Bikana International Ltd of Zambia; this brought the consortium's holding to 82%, with the remaining 18% transferred to the Zambia Privatisation Trust Fund.[9] In 2006/7 General Cable Corporation, a US-based manufacturer of aluminium and fibreoptic wire and cable

[7] *Source*: www.thebestofzambia.com.

[8] Zambia Privatisation Agency. 2001. *Status Report* (31 December).

[9] Zambia Privatisation Agency. 2000. *Zambia Privatisation: A Progress Report,* No. 17 (December).

products, took over; General Cable Corporation now holds 55.24% of the company's shares through its wholly owned subsidiary Phelps Dodge Africa Cable Corporation. The remaining shares were floated on the Lusaka Stock Exchange. General Cable Corporation also acquired two companies in South Africa that act as a marketing and distribution arm for ZAMEFA.

Current activities and products. ZAMEFA buys copper cathode from mines and smelts it down to copper rods, cables and wires. The company produces bare copper wires, low-voltage power cables, aluminum–steel reinforced overhead conductors, building wires, flexible cables, and telecommunication wire.

Organization and management. The CEO of ZAMEFA reports to the General Cable Corporation managing director for sub-Saharan Africa, who in turn reports to the executive president of General Cable Corporation. The board of directors of ZAMEFA meets once or twice every quarter.

Supply and marketing chain. ZAMEFA buys copper from Konkola Copper Mines and Mopani, the nearby mines, which provide high-quality copper. A mine in Luanshya is now operating under new Chinese owners; it has opened three pits and begun producing copper cathodes and it could, in time, offer a third source of supply to ZAMEFA.

ZAMEFA imports aluminum from South Africa and China, and plastic compounds for insulation from Mauritius, Malaysia, the US, South Africa and Europe.

About 35% of the company's output is sold domestically, mainly to ZESCO but also to the Zambia Telecommunications Company ZAMTEL, the mines and the Copperbelt Energy Corporation. ZAMEFA has a showroom in Lusaka and it also sells through select agents.

A challenge for ZAMEFA is that locally based Chinese companies with investment licenses are given duty and tax concessions when they bring in finished copper wire. ZAMEFA does not receive concessions, however, when it imports aluminum and the plastic compound it needs for wire insulation. The company is calling for a level playing field and advocating a policy change.

ZAMEFA does not have any domestic competition in copper rods, cables and wires, but it foresees that there may be competition from Chinese firms entering the market in future.

Exports. Some 85% of the company's sales revenue derives from exports. ZAMEFA's primary export market is South Africa, but it also exports to

Kenya, the Democratic Republic of the Congo, Botswana, Namibia and Europe.

Development agenda. ZAMEFA is now making copper shapes and is assessing the potential for manufacturing fibreoptics and possibly minting now that the currency has lost three zeros and coins have been reintroduced. ZAMEFA is exploring the possibility of setting up local companies capable of producing aluminium and plastic to reduce imports and streamline their entire operation.

13.2.2 Good Time Steel Company Limited (GTS)

Basic details. GTS has an annual turnover of US$30 million; it exports approximately 40% of its production.

It has around 550 employees, and the company expects to increase total employment to 700 staff in the near future as its production of angle iron bars and window frames comes on stream.

History. GTS was established in 2005 and began operations in 2008 in a greenfield factory using equipment and expertise from China. The company was formed to fill a gap in the market as there were no local steel companies at that time.

Current activities and products. GTS makes re-bar and plans to expand into angle iron bars in late 2012; it also has plans to make metal tubes in 2013.

Most of the company's equipment comes from China, with some machines also sourced from Germany and South Africa. Technicians were hired from China as, according to GTS, workers with suitable skills were not available locally.

Organization and management. The company has a three-person board of directors and a general manager who reports to the board; it also has three deputy managers and one senior engineer.

Firm capabilities. GTS is operating at its full capacity, producing around 30,000 mt of re-bar annually, typically in 12 m lengths.

Supply and marketing chain. Mild steel scrap is the primary input, and this is sourced locally. Chemicals (ferromanganese and silicon) are imported from South Africa.

Another challenge is the lack of skilled labour. The factory should be able to operate with a workforce of 100 or 150 but there are not enough skilled workers available, reflecting a lack of local training programmes to develop the skills required for maintenance of precision machinery. This forces the company to continue recruiting Chinese technical personnel.

GTS is working with the Zambian Development Agency and the Ministry of Commerce, Trade and Industry to develop a plan that includes recommendations on training Zambians to work in highly skilled positions. Currently, according to GTS, it takes 3–5 years to fully train a Zambian worker.

Domestically, GTS sells to construction companies and small businesses.

Exports. GTS exports to Burundi, Namibia, Zimbabwe and Mozambique.

Development agenda. GTS is looking to expand into angle iron (for window frames, for example) and metal tubes because these products are in demand from their re-bar clients. GTS has the necessary capacity, but it needs additional technology and knowhow. The company is also planning to become a shareholder in a new cement plant in Ndola.

The expansion programme aims to turn the company into a one-stop shop for the construction industry. To accomplish this aim it also plans to acquire a coal mine, using coal as the fuel for extracting iron from iron ore and for cement production. GTS is also hoping to establish its own construction company.

13.2.3 Universal Mining and Chemical Industries Limited (Kafue Steel)[10]

Basic details. Kafue Steel is a recently opened steel refinery making deformed bar, angle iron and flat bar from scrap metal. It employs 800 workers and had a turnover of US$36–40 million in 2011.

History. UMCIL was incorporated in 1989 as a joint venture between Universal Bakeries Ltd, which is part of the Trade Kings conglomerate,[11] and Dr Julius Kaoma, who is the executive technical director of the company. Dr Kaoma began his career as a government employee, working at the National Institute for Scientific and Industrial Research.[12]

The company sought opportunities that take advantage of local raw materials, particularly copper. An initial plan to produce copper oxychloride fungicide was unsuccessful because local copper was sold at

[10] Kafue Steel is the only business currently operating within UMCIL.

[11] More precisely, the individual shareholders in Trade Kings Ltd are also the majority shareholders in UMCIL.

[12] Dr Kaoma is pictured on the front cover of this book (on the right-hand side).

London Metal Exchange (LME) prices; foreign exchange was scarce at the time and the market proved difficult to penetrate due to the presence of multinational agrochemical companies.

The company then explored alternative opportunities, including the manufacture of plasterboard and plaster of Paris using a gypsum deposit, but no finance could be raised.

In 2001 the partners decided to embark on their current venture in steel making. Various plans had been formulated over the years to establish a steel producer in Zambia. The possibility was explored in 1968 by the Zambian government but the project never came to fruition. In 1980/81 the Indeco group of companies approached the Indian conglomerate Tata and evaluated the commercial case for manufacturing steel from scrap, but again the project did not come to fruition.

Then, in 1988, the Zambian government approached the government of the USSR to explore the issue and a detailed feasibility study was prepared. An agreement appeared to be in sight, but the events of 1991 and its aftermath led to the plan being dropped. The feasibility study, which was accessible to third parties, did however play a key role in UMCIL's new venture. The study described an integrated project, involving iron ore extraction through a rolling mill. The project would be located at Kabwe (which had good rail links) or Kafue (near Lusaka). It was the plan set out in this study that would form the basis of UMCIL's new venture.

A 81 acre site at Kafue was acquired from the National Housing Authority, with finance raised from the Trade Kings group. The collection and accumulation of a store of scrap steel began in 2004. Construction of a factory on the site began in 2006, with a steel making plant, including a rolling mill, sourced from India. Phase I of the operation opened in 2008, with an annual production volume of 100,000 mt.

The process was not without setbacks. In December 2008 a reactor/transformer unit failed, leading to a four-month halt in production. When production recommenced in April 2009, the firm was producing angles, flat bars and profile ('channel'), but it was unable to generate sales and the company was therefore stockpiling most of what it produced. Competition from Chinese producers (GTS and the now-non-operational Millennium Steel) who had been operating in Zambia since 2008 was extremely tough. UMCIL's main problem lay in perceptions about the quality of its products: buyers were unwilling to trust a Zambian steel maker. The key turning point in the firm's fortunes came after it obtained a series of quality certifications, first from the Zambian authorities in respect of its re-bar and then from the South African Bureau of Standards (SANS 920 for re-bar in 2010 and

SANS 14301 for long sections in 2011). This led to a major jump in sales and placed the operation on a secure commercial footing.

The plant commenced operations in 2008 but technical problems stalled production until 2009.

Current activities and products. UMCIL produces d-bar and long sections, angles, channel and flat bars.

In 2012 production was approximately 80% deformed bar and 20% other long sections in the form of channels, angles, strips and flat bar. The company was aiming to reach its full capacity of 100,000 mt per annum in 2012.

Organization and management. Until 2012 the management of UMCIL followed a style of management used within the Trade Kings group, under which executive directors, who are members of the shareholding family, are assigned specific tasks. In 2012 UMCIL adopted a more formal management structure, with the employment of a professional managing director from outside the family; the board does still consist of family members, however.

Firm capabilities. The first phase of the company's plans is now fully operational and the firm is embarking on Phase II (see below).

Supply and marketing chain. UMCIL began accumulating scrap in 2004 and had stockpiled about 120,000 mt by 2008. It currently has around 50,000 mt of scrap that it uses as raw material.

Exports. In 2010 the company had production of 20,000 mt, 40% of which was exported. In 2011 production rose to 50,000 mt, with 60% being exported. The main export destinations are South Africa, Mozambique, Malawi, Tanzania and Burundi.

Development agenda. Phase II of the project, which is now under way, aims at backward integration into mining. The plan involves the opening up of the Sanje iron ore mine, located 45 km from the firm's site at Kafue. The company has already signed a contract with the Zambian government to build a road from the mine. It hoped to begin mining iron ore in 2013. This venture will represent a major advance for steel making in Zambia, with steel being made from iron ore rather than scrap for the first time. A third phase of the project, which will involve the production of ferroalloy, is envisaged to follow.

13.2.4 Kavino Limited

Basic details. Kavino produces drawn wire, copper cables and galvanized roofing sheet. It employs 160 people.

History. The firm was founded in 1994 by the current managing director's father, the late Mr O. P. Saxena, as a family business involved in the trading of drawn wire, imported from South Africa and Zimbabwe, and construction steel products (angle iron and deformed bars), imported from South Africa, Kenya and Mozambique. As the economy improved, the firm began manufacturing roofing sheets and nails in 1997, cables in 2006, and door frames in 2007.

The firm first began manufacturing drawn wire in response to the long and uncertain delivery times it experienced from its South African suppliers, and to the economic turmoil in Zimbabwe, its other source of supply.

The company also had an informal relationship with Tata International of India for the supply of galvanized iron pipes and coils.

Current activities and products. Kavino has four lines of business: manufacturing of cables, semi-manufacturing of roofing sheets, production of wire nails and window and door frames, and trading in construction steel (angle iron and deformed bars).

Organization and management. The company is overseen by its family owners, together with a professional operations manager who is a mechanical engineer.

Firm capabilities. Kavino produces around 300 mt of copper cable per annum, 8,000 mt of roofing sheets per annum, 2 mt of nails per day, and 2,000–3,000 door frames per month.

Its copper wire meets South African Bureau of Standards and ZABS requirements.

Supply and marketing chain. Kavino sources copper rods in coil form from ZAMEFA and from the Zinc Aluminum Lead and Copper Company Ltd; it also sometimes imports supplies from South Africa. (Prices are based on LME prices.)

Iron sheets are bought in coil form from South Africa to manufacture roofing sheets.

Production is to customer order and the company mostly focuses on the local market, in which it claims a share of 35–40% for copper cables, largely supplied to the construction industry.

Exports. Kavino exports drawn wire to Malawi and the Democratic Republic of the Congo. It also exports copper cables indirectly through traders who export to Zimbabwe, the Democratic Republic of the Congo, Mozambique and Malawi.

Recent developments. The company began making heavy-duty high-tensile industrial cables in 2011 to expand its product base.

Chapter 14

CHEMICALS AND PHARMACEUTICALS

14.1 Sector Profile

Background and overview. The Zambian chemical industry is involved in the production of sulphuric acid, explosives, detonators, cosmetics and industrial gases. Other products are automotive batteries, soaps and detergents, ferrosilicon, talcum powder, polyvinyl acetate and gloss paints, fertilizers and industrial/mining batteries.

Zambia's chemical industry contributed about 11% to the country's total manufacturing revenue in the early 1990s. Due to limited natural petroleum resources, Zambia has a largely imported oil industry and consequently has little petrochemical activity.

Chemical and pharmaceutical products contributed US$90 million (6%) to non-traditional export earnings in 2010 according to the Zambia Development Agency's *Exporter Audit Report* of 2010 (Table 14.1).

There are six officially registered manufacturers of pharmaceutical products.

Three are based in Lusaka: Pharmanova (Z) Ltd, which makes tablets and capsules, and liquid oral preparations; International Drug Company Ltd, which makes tablets and capsules, topical preparations and liquid oral preparations; and Tejay Pharmaceuticals Ltd, which makes injectibles and liquid oral preparations. International Drug Company also has operations in Kabwe—these are treated as a separate manufacturing entity by the Pharmaceutical Regulatory Authority (PRA)—where it makes intravenous fluids.

In Ndola, Baxy Pharmaceuticals Manufacturing Company Ltd makes tablets and capsules, penicillins, injectibles and liquid oral preparations.

A sixth company, VYKing Pharmaceuticals Ltd, has notified the PRA that it will be closing operations.

The Society for Family Health was also originally classified as a manufacturing company but it has since been reclassified as an importer and wholesale dealer as it merely packages manufactured medicines into

TABLE 14.1. Chemical and pharmaceutical export earnings, 2005–10 (all figures in thousands of US$; nominal prices).

2005	2006	2007	2008	2009	2010
20,572	20,224	38,315	93,332	76,744	90,335

Source: Exporter Audit Report 2010, Zambia Development Agency.

blister packs. Pharmaceutical products in Zambia are regulated by the Pharmaceutical Act No. 14 of 2004. The act established the PRA, which is responsible for the registration and regulation of pharmacies and the registration and regulation of medicines, herbal medicines and allied substances intended for human use and for animal use. It also controls the manufacture, importation, exportation, possession, storage, distribution, supply, promotion, sale and use of medicines.

The government, through the Ministry of Health, is involved in the industry through the procurement of pharmaceuticals for all government health institutions in Zambia. This is done by the Procurement and Supplies Unit of the Ministry of Health, which is funded by the government itself and by cooperating partners.

Churches Health Association of Zambia is also involved in supply management as a complement to the government supply system. With support from cooperating partners, it runs antiretroviral therapy and malaria treatment programmes, which include procurement, storage and distribution of medicines.

There are 125 retail pharmacists in the country, 80 pharmaceutical importers/wholesalers and 300 private dispensing clinics with one or two doctors each. No more than 30,000–50,000 Zambians are privately insured. The limited size of the retail sector means that local pharmaceutical firms have a very small domestic market.

According to a 2010 survey carried out by PRA, 78.9% of all medical products are imported. Some 61% of imported products come from India.

Policy context. Imported medical products are cheaper than domestically manufactured ones; they are duty free and zero-rated for VAT. Manufacturing companies in Zambia pay tax on materials, packaging and other inputs, making their products more expensive. Since imported chemicals can be used in illicit manufacturing, controlled products require clearance from the PRA. Another statutory body, the Drug Enforcement Commission, monitors the use of imported chemicals.

Profiles and lines of business of large firms. The major firms in the chemicals and pharmaceuticals sector include Indeni Petroleum, Afrox Zambia Limited, Nitrogen Chemicals of Zambia and Ndola Lime, all of which are profiled in the next section.

Others players in the industry are Trade Kings Limited, Dyno Nobel Zambia Limited, Nasla Chemicals Limited, Vitafro Limited, Vitretex Paints, Churches Health Association of Zambia, African Explosives Zambia PLC, Bwana Mkubwa Mining Limited, Chloride Zambia Limited and Plascon Paints Zambia Limited.

An important part of chemicals exports comes from the mining sector, and especially from Mopani Copper Mine and Chambishi Copper Mine (Chapter 16). Sino-Acid Products Zambia Limited and Sino-Metal Leach Company Limited are affiliated to the Chambishi Copper Mine and operate within the Zambia–China Economic and Trade Co-operation Zone (Chapter 1). Exports from this sector include anode slime and sulphuric acid.

Indeni Petroleum is Zambia's only oil refinery. It is profiled in the next section.

Afrox Zambia Limited produces industrial gases. It is profiled in the next section.

Nitrogen Chemicals of Zambia produces explosives and fertilizers. It is profiled in the next section.

Ndola Lime Company Limited was founded in 1931 as Northern Rhodesia Lime Company Limited. The only producer of lime in the Copperbelt, it produces limestone, quicklime and hydrated lime. It is profiled in the next section.

African Explosives Zambia Plc makes and distributes commercial explosives, initiating systems and blasting services. It's turnover for the year to 20 June 2012 was US$1.9 million.[1]

The company began operations in 1963 with production of anflex explosives.

African Explosives Zambia is a subsidiary of AEL Mining Services Zambia, a member of the AECI Ltd group in South Africa. AECI operates in Africa and Indonesia and is a leading developer, producer and supplier of commercial explosives, initiating systems and blasting services. AECI holds an 80% stake in AEL Mining Services Zambia.

[1] African explosives record. *Zambia Daily Mail*, 14 September 2012.

African Explosives Zambia is based near Mufulira in the Copperbelt but it also has a manufacturing plant in Lumwana. The company supplies shaft head deliveries of explosives and initiating systems. It operates underground bulk explosives mobile pumping units and offers down-the-hole services for surface mining operations. It also operates a fleet of mobile manufacturing units and provides engineering and technical support through a customer services unit.

In 2009 the company commissioned a manufacturing plant to make bulk emulsion explosives, a low-cost alternative to watergel and fuel oil explosives, at the Equinox Mineral copper mine in Lumwana, with which it has a ten-year contract for the manufacture and supply of explosives.

Trade Kings Limited is engaged in the manufacture and production of detergents, soaps, washing power and confectionery. It is profiled in Chapter 2.

Profiles and lines of business of medium-sized firms.

International Chemicals Limited was established in 1968, primarily to manufacture pharmaceutical products and cosmetics. It employs 40 permanent and 20 casual workers. The firm is a private limited liability company generating an annual turnover of US$1 million. It has an asset value of US$4 million.

International Chemicals has a board of directors consisting of six major shareholders. The chairman, who is one of the six, is the head of the board and acts as CEO. Line management includes a general manager, a sales manager and a chief accountant.

The firm produces hair products (shampoo, conditioner, gel, pomade), Medix rub-on (which is a body jelly rubbed on the body to relieve muscular pain) and veterinary products. It also imports raw materials and finished pharmaceuticals from India and the UK.

The firm has created strong relationships with suppliers and customers.

The company indirectly exports by reselling its imported products to countries within the SADC region. The company operates its own fleet of vehicles to distribute its products.

Handyman's Paradise Limited is also reported to have embarked on the construction of a US$45 million quicklime plant in Masaiti in the Copperbelt, with a production capacity of 300–500 mt per day and 30 staff.[2]

[2] Handyman's embarks on $45m lime project. *Zambia Daily Mail*, 4 June 2012.

Small-scale, informal and peripheral activities. There are various small and informal enterprises in Zambia that are involved in chemical and pharmaceutical activities but they do not manufacture.

Supply and marketing chain. Limestone is sourced locally from Ndola Lime Company and is used in the manufacture of fertilizer, cement and glass.

Export status and potential. All key export markets for Zambia in this sector are regional, with growing demand in the Democratic Republic of the Congo, Zimbabwe, Malawi, Tanzania, South Africa and Botswana.[3]

Products exported to SADC countries, the Democratic Republic of the Congo, Zimbabwe, Malawi, Tanzania, South Africa and Botswana include argon gas, sulphuric acid, detonators, automotive batteries, paints, cosmetics, soaps and detergents.

Policy context. Pharmaceuticals in Zambia are regulated by the PRA through the National Drug Policy. Policy formulation, procurement and standards for use on the Zambian market are the responsibilities of the Ministry of Health with cooperating partners: the Zambia Public Procurement Authority and National Drug Policy. Storage and distribution of pharmaceutical and medical supplies is undertaken by National Medical Stores, a government parastatal owned by the Ministry of Finance and the Ministry of Health.

All firms involved in the production and distribution of pharmaceuticals are legally required to be registered and licensed with the PRA and the Ministry of Health. This process ensures that all pharmaceutical products meet with World Health Organization guidelines and practices.

There is no special policy on generic drugs. Their sale is permitted as long as they meet Zambian quality standards. Policies concerning good manufacturing practice for domestic and foreign manufacturers are defined in the Pharmaceutical Act of 2004.

A number of individuals operate illegal practices selling out-of-date medicines. These unregulated and informal chemists, pharmacies, drug stores or clinics pose a challenge to regulating authorities and can threaten health.

Challenges. Promotion of medical products is strictly controlled and requires permission from regulatory authorities including the Ministry of Health. Enforcement of such laws and monitoring adherence is difficult, however, due to limited capacity.

[3] Zambia Development Agency. 2012. *Directory of Zambian Exporters 2011.*

Unregistered chemicals and medicaments enter the local market without being monitored and these pose dangers to consumers.

All new medicines entering the country should in principle be sample-tested by the Food and Drugs Laboratory. However, this often does not happen in practice, given the limited resources available to the laboratory.

Certain pharmaceutical products specified under the Basic Health Care Package are, in principle, available free of charge at health centres and district hospitals, though in practice there may be a charge for some of these items. In the private sector, which has been fully liberalized since 1991, prices vary but they are usually higher than those in government health centres and district hospitals.

14.2 Profiles of Major Firms

14.2.1 Indeni Petroleum Limited

Basic details. Indeni Petroleum, which is government owned, is Zambia's only refiner of crude oil, producing heavy fuel oil, automotive gas oil (diesel), Jet A-1, industrial and domestic kerosene, petrol, butane and liquefied petroleum gas (LPG).

Its turnover was US$39 million in 2011. It employs 300 people.

History. At independence, Zambia relied on southern links for imports, including fuel. In 1965 the Southern Rhodesian government closed the southern trade route. The Zambian government was faced with rising demand for fuel as industrialization continued. To try and mitigate the situation, fuel was airlifted to Ndola airport, before a northern rail route with Tanzania was finally established along the Tazara Railway. The government began investigating ways of enhancing fuel supply, and in the late 1960s construction of the Tanzania Zambia Mafuta (TAZAMA) pipeline began. This pipeline transported finished petroleum products into the National Oil Supply Company in the Bwana Mkubwa industrial area of Ndola. Then, in the early 1970s, the Zambian government—through Zambia's INDECO—decided to build a refinery and sought partners in Europe. Investment partners were found in the Italian Eni state group under Agip management, and the partnership gave rise to the name Indeni. The Italian engineering firm Bercel was contracted to build an oil refinery in Ndola and construction was completed in 1973. The TAZAMA pipeline was converted to carry crude oil, where before it had only transported finished products (including kerosene and petrol).

In 2002 TotalFinaElf (one of the world's major oil and gas groups, now named Total) acquired the refining and marketing assets of Agip Zambia, an Agip (Eni group) subsidiary, which included a 50% stake in Indeni. In 2009 Total sold its share to the Zambian government, making the company 100% government owned.

Current activities and products. The Indeni Petroleum refinery processes 700,000 mt of crude oil per annum. It produces a range of petroleum products including heavy fuel oil, automotive gas oil (diesel), Jet A-1, industrial and domestic kerosene, petrol, butane and LPG.

Organization and management. The company managing director is Maybin Noole. The firm is run by a team of local experts trained in engineering, finance, legal administration and technical production. The board is appointed by the Minister of Energy. Neither the company managing director nor the employees are civil servants: they are all employed directly by Indeni Petroleum.

Firm capabilities. The Indeni Petroleum plant allows for processing of 1.1 million mt of crude oil per annum. Plant modifications and the boosting of feedstock, in particular the restoration of the company's bitumen facility, are expected to see the plant running at full capacity in early 2013. Consumption losses occur in the refining process—sometimes excess water has to be drained—but new and more efficient technology is being researched to reduce consumption loss from 14% to below 7%.

Supply and marketing chain. Petroleum feedstock is sourced from the Middle East and the Arabian Gulf by the Zambian government. Indeni Petroleum is paid a processing fee. Chemicals used in the refining process are imported from South Africa and the Netherlands. Marketing is handled by the government agency TAZAMA Petroleum Products Limited.

Indeni Petroleum is Zambia's sole refinery and as such has no competition, with demand outstripping supply. This may change, though, as private investors are exploring the option of building a new refinery. The refinery has faced some calls for closure from the Zambia Institute for Policy Analysis and Research, on the grounds that most products supplied by Indeni Petroleum are already imported. The advantage of keeping it running, however, comes in the form of halved transportation and freight costs: the cost of processing combined with importing the crude oil is less than US$100 per mt, against US$200 per mt on imports of refined products from Dar es Salaam.

Recent developments. The refinery has been implementing a US$65 million recapitalization programme in the last three years. This programme has resulted in an overhaul of key refinery infrastructure including furnaces and reactors, paid for by the Zambian government, which has in turn resulted in healthier returns. Indeni Petroleum's bitumen plant, closed in 2005 due to low market demand, is currently being refurbished and the vacuum unit revamped to resume production in 2013. The company is also in the process of acquiring a light gasoline isomerizer at an estimated cost of US$10 million and a gas oil hydrotreater at an estimated cost of US$20 million. Once these have been procured, there is a proposal in place to acquire a mild hydrocracker so that the refinery can process crude oil, which is cheaper than the current commingled feedstock (which is a crude oil base that has gas oil or naphta added to it to formulate either gasoline or petroleum).

14.2.2 Trade Kings Limited

The Trade Kings group consists of eight entities, including one that manufactures detergents, soaps and washing power (see Chapter 2).

14.2.3 Nitrogen Chemicals of Zambia Limited (NCZ)

Basic details. NCZ makes a fertilizer known as basal dressing fertilizer (a mix of nitrogen, phosphorous and potash) that is used in maize farming. (It is also known as NPK.)

NCZ supplies 20% of government fertilizer contracts. It has a workforce of 450 full-time employees. Its 2011 turnover was US$30 million.

History. NCZ was established in 1970, with Japanese assistance (from Kobe Steel), to supply explosive grade ammonium nitrate to the mines through Explosives Kafironda Limited. Its operations were enhanced in 1982 with the addition of a manufacturing plant for fertilizer under the auspices of Germany's Klockner-ina.

The principal activity of NCZ since its inception has been the manufacture of, and trade in, explosive grade ammonium nitrate, chemicals, fertilizers and industrial chemicals. It provides ammonium nitrate explosive to the mines and chemical fertilizer and some industrial chemicals to the agricultural sector. It has also been engaged in the trading of manufactured products.

The company has been wholly owned by government since its inception in 1970, but it is now earmarked for privatization.

Current activities and products. The company has a basal fertilizer production capacity of 30,000 mt per annum.

Organization and management. The firm has a board of directors that appoints management. The CEO is appointed by the board and is responsible for making operational decisions. The members are all civil servants and are appointed by government.

Firm capabilities. NCZ is a viable entity that makes an important contribution to the agriculture sector. The firm's top management are well trained and are experienced. NCZ's government contracts are on attractive terms, allowing it to finance its other operations.

However, despite growing demand for mining and industrial chemicals, the firm has not been able to work at full capacity and has operated at a loss. Inadequate funding and dilapidated infrastructure have affected its potential to meet market demand and develop its business.

Supply and marketing chain. The firm sources sulphates and nitrogen from South Africa, North Africa and Eastern Europe.

Basal fertilizer is distributed to local markets by the company's own fleet of trucks. Some buyers collect directly from the plant.

Recent developments. The firm's major focus is on upgrading its plant to improve productivity.

Development agenda. The firm intends to restore production lines that have not been operational for some time. In particular, it intends to recommission its ammonium nitrate plant.

14.2.4 Afrox Zambia Limited

Basic details. Afrox Zambia is a supplier of industrial gases to industrial and medical users. Based in Ndola and Lusaka, it employed 180 people in 2009 and had a turnover of US$15 million.

History. The origins of Afrox Zambia can be traced to a small company, Ailen Liversedge Limited, that began in 1927 producing oxygen and acetylene. It was renamed as the Northern Rhodesia Oxygen and Acetylene Company Ltd in 1931. In 1939 the company was again renamed as the

Northern Rhodesia Co, and BOC, the British multinational industrial gases company, became a shareholder.

Following independence the company was renamed Zamox in 1968. Zamox was subsequently nationalized, but BOC retained a minority share through its London office.

In 1996 the company was privatized. BOC sold its minority stake and the business was bought by Afrox, the South African subsidiary of BOC.

In 2006 BOC sold its interests to Linde, the German multinational supplier of industrial gases. Afrox Zambia is currently 70% owned by Linde and 30% owned by the Zambian government.

Current activities and products. Afrox's main products are oxygen and acetylene, for which the main customers are mining companies. Its second biggest line of business involves the supply of carbon dioxide to the beverages industries. It also supplies cylinders of LPG directly to households. It has a small business supplying oxygen to hospitals—this accounts for 2% of sales revenue. The company also supplies welding accessories, including electrodes—this accounts for 10% of total sales.

Organization and management. The company has a managing director at its headquarters in Kitwe who is appointed by Afrox management and a regional manager in its other branch in Lusaka. Its other departments include human resources, corporate affairs and accounts.

Firm capabilities. Afrox operates a single large-scale air separation facility in Ndola that supplies all its air separation products. It also has a plant for compressed acetylene in Ndola. It produces carbon dioxide and LPG in Lusaka.

Supply and marketing chain. Afrox sources LPG from Indeni Petroleum, the domestic oil refinery, but also imports some LPG from South Africa. Some 75% of its sales comprise gases in cylinders, which are transported by the company's fleet of trucks.

Exports. Exports account for 9% of total sales. The company has a branch in the Democratic Republic of the Congo that supplies oxygen in liquid form to Zimbabwe and Malawi, using road tankers. It also supplies LPG to Malawi.

Competition. Afrox is the dominant supplier of industrial gases in Zambia and is the only company in the country that is a subsidiary of one of the five major multinationals who dominate the industry worldwide. It faces competition in Zambia from a number of newly arrived Chinese companies in the supply of oxygen, and from the Indian-owned firm Oxyzam, based in Lusaka. One Chinese company, Chinogas, is active in the supply of oxygen to medical users.

Recent developments. The government has encouraged the use of LPG for environmental reasons and this has led to significant growth in the LPG market.

Since 2005 Afrox has been developing a business in the supply of safety products (safety boots, protective clothing and underground safety devices for mines) but this market remain small and competition is intense.

14.2.5 Ndola Lime Company Limited (NLC)

Basic details. NLC is a wholly owned subsidiary of ZCCM Investments Holdings Plc. The company produces lime, limestone and quicklime. It is based in Ndola and employs 427 permanent workers.

History. The company was founded in 1931 as the Northern Rhodesia Lime Company Limited under an agreement between the Rhokana Corporation Limited and Ndola engineer John Owen Wallen to supply lime to the mines. Its initial lime burning trials were carried out in wood-fired, hollowed-out anthills. The lime burning trials yielded positive results and this led to the construction of underground pot kilns. A second quarry was opened in the 1930s at Chipulukusu before the company moved to its present location at Mwatesi in 1962.

In 1973 a rotary kiln was commissioned and in 1986 a 500 mt per day annular vertical kiln was added to cater for increased lime demand, especially at the tailing leach plant in Chingola.

Current activities and products. NLC quarries limestone, which is then crushed and screened into aggregates of various sizes. The limestone serves as the raw material for quicklime production.

The company produced about 174,000 mt of quicklime in 2011, which was the highest production volume that the company has achieved since 1996.

Organization and management. NLC has a board of directors that appoints the CEO and other directors that cover quality assurance, accounts, information and communications technology, production, engineering, human resources, marketing and sales, supply and internal auditing.

The CEO heads the company but does so in consultation with other senior managers. All departments are managed by professionals.

Firm capabilities. Rocks are reduced and graded in a series of crushers and vibrating screens and then stored in silos for use in its smelters and kilns. Some 10% of the quicklime produced is further processed into hydrated lime.

Supply and marketing chain. The firm provides limestone from its own quarry. Lime is used in cement and fertilizer manufacturing, coal mining, the building industry and for leather tanning.

Exports. The company exports its products to Zimbabwe, Malawi, the Democratic Republic of the Congo and to other SADC countries.

Recent developments. A fully automated hydrating plant supplied by Cimprogetti of Italy was completed in October 2011.

Development agenda. The firm intends to install a new vertical kiln for quicklime production with a capacity of 500 mt per day. This dual fired kiln will run on both heavy fuel oil and coal (which is a relatively cheap fuel source).

Operation of this kiln in conjunction with refurbished existing plants will push annual quicklime output from the current 170,000 mt per annum to over 300,000 mt.

Chapter 15

PLASTICS AND GLASS

15.1 Sector Profile

Background and overview. The Zambian plastics sector produces pipes, household ware and packaging. While there is some overlap between the firms that manufacture pipes and those that produce household ware, the three operations are generally undertaken by different specialized companies. Packaging is often made in-house as part of a vertical integration strategy by food processing and beverage manufacturers.

Most glass is imported, with only one domestic manufacturer, Kapiri Glass Products, which is now attempting to recover from a prolonged period when it has not been operative.

Structure of the plastics industry. Plastic products can be split into three types: pipes for water and sewage, household plasticware, and bottles and packaging.

Historically, pipe manufacturers such as Lamasat International Zambia Ltd began by servicing the mines and winning government contracts. Lamasat International Zambia is also active in agricultural irrigation.

Demand for household plasticware has grown with the economy in recent years, with manufacturers importing granules and using a variety of moulds to create buckets, basins, plates, bowls, plastic chairs and tables, and storage items. They face competition from imported products, often from China or Kenya (Table 15.1).

The manufacture of plastic bottles and packaging has often been driven by companies setting out to vertically integrate their production processes because they find it easier and more economical to produce their packaging in-house. In the bottled water industry, for example, preformed bottles are usually imported and blown on site.

Manufacturers of polyethylene bags, woven polypropylene bags and sheeting serve the grain and food processing industries.

TABLE 15.1. Domestic demand: imports of manufactured plastic articles from COMESA and the SADC (all figures in thousands of US$).

	2007	2008	2009
COMESA	5,707	6,495	6,645
SADC	95,507	100,661	86,355

Source: Zambia Development Agency. 2011. *Manufacturing: Sector Profile* (February).

Supply and marketing chain. Plastic granules are imported from South Africa and Asia. (Asian imports are favoured by those companies who buy in large quantities.)

Pipes are sold direct to end users such as farms and construction companies, or are supplied under tender to government or mines.

Household ware is often sold from factory outlets to traders and retailers who distribute to smaller outlets. A similar arrangement is common for plastic bags and packaging.

Bottles are generally imported by end users as preforms from South Africa.

Policy context. The industry anticipates a growing focus on environmental issues relating to degradability and disposal of plastic products.

Challenges. The plastics business has been suffering from a serious decline in output since mid 2011. Firms that were previously operating 24 hours a day, seven days a week are now typically operating five days a week, producing about 70% of the monthly volumes of early 2011. There are, however, no immediate plans to change course or cut the workforce.

The government's FRA buys a reported 28 million grain bags a year, usually through traders, but problems with supply have recently prompted the FRA to approach manufacturers directly.

The manufacturers have called for protection from Chinese imports, and have expressed regret at the lack of an industry association. They attribute this in part to the wide range of ethnic cultures and origins of the different plastics companies.

Export status and potential. Almost all the industry's output goes to the domestic market, but there are some informal cross-border traders who buy in Zambia and sell in the Democratic Republic of the Congo and elsewhere.

Competitiveness. Competition is mainly from Malawi and Tanzania, which have lower costs and, therefore, prices. There is little direct competition from China for basic household plasticware as it is too expensive to ship finished goods.

The manufacturers of plastic and woven bags, however, are finding it difficult to compete on price with imports from China, which sell at a third of the price of locally produced bags and offer a whiter colour, thanks to better Chinese manufacturing technology.

Profiles and lines of business of large firms. Lamasat International Zambia is estimated to be the largest manufacturer of plastic products overall, with a market share of around 30% in the polypropylene woven bags sector; Polythene Products Zambia Limited and Habib Industries Ltd account for around 15% of the sector each. Acton Plastics Ltd, Sakiza Spinning Ltd and Kifco together account for the remainder. Lamise Investments Limited manufactures household items.

Profiles and lines of business of medium-sized firms. Kazuma Plastics has 42 employees and a turnover of US$120,000 per month, which includes income from both plastics and steel roof sheets. The company has been in operation since 1998, when the family bought a plastics company in Kafue that had been making recreational boats. Fibreglass vessels are still part of the firm's output.

The company began by manufacturing three lines: fibreglass tanks, commercial fibreglass boats and translucent roof sheeting. It also offered repairs. Later, the company began to manufacture water tanks and rolling roofing sheets.

All raw materials are imported from South Africa: fibreglass, plastics and steel. The company buys finished products for resale from Lamasat International Zambia and Imperial Plastics. Kazuma Plastics does not export. Its main domestic competitors are Lamasat International Zambia and Roto Tanks.

Glass manufacturing: Kapiri Glass Products Limited. Kapiri Glass Products is Zambia's only glass manufacturer but it has been moribund since 1998. Attempts are now under way to revive the business.

Kapiri Glass Products was established by the government in the 1960s and was a government parastatal until it was privatized in October 1995, at which point it employed 219 people.

Under the privatization, some 89% of the company was sold under preemption rights to Floco Verwaltungs-und Beteiligungsgesellschaft MBH (a German investment company that was an existing minority shareholder) for US$1.4 million plus liabilities and an investment commitment of US$7 million, bringing Floco Verwaltungs-und Beteiligungsgesellschaft MBH's shareholding to 98%. The remaining 2% of shares are held by the Zambia National Provident Fund.[1]

Kapiri Glass Products went into receivership in 1997 and its assets were bought in 2008 by local entrepreneur Costain Chilala. Mr Chilala is attempting to resuscitate the original factory and revive the business under the name Kapiri Glass Manufacturing Ltd with the help of an US$8m loan from PTA Bank.

The management of the company is handled by Costain Chilala through his family's Chimsoro group of companies.

The company is expected to resume full production in 2013 with an initial production capacity of 75 mt of glass a day; thereafter it plans to expand capacity to 100 mt per day. Kapiri Glass Manufacturing has partnered with equipment suppliers from Switzerland, Italy and Germany that specialize in glassmaking equipment.

Construction and rehabilitation of the company's factory is due for completion in 2013 after the company signed an US$8 million loan agreement with PTA Bank in January 2012 to revive the plant. The project is expected to create over 400 jobs. The new plant is expected to cost US$22 million, of which US$13.6 million is working capital. Of this total US$13.6 million, the company has sourced US$8 million from PTA Bank, another US$2 million from the Development Bank of Zambia, and the remainder will be funded by the Chimsoro group of companies, which is owned by the Chilala family.

15.2 Profiles of Major Firms

15.2.1 Lamasat International Zambia Ltd

Basic details. Lamasat International Zambia makes a range of plastic products, as well as aluminium products and furniture. It employs around 1,200 staff.

History. Lamasat International Zambia is part of a wider group of businesses that are owned and run by five Lebanese brothers. Lamasat International Zambia was registered in 2002. The brothers' other businesses include Lamise Investments Limited (profiled below) and Batul, which makes biscuits.

[1] Zambia Development Agency. 2012. *Privatisation Status Report as of January 31, 2012.*

Lamasat International Zambia was established in Zambia by Mohammed Ahmed, who was involved in trading and in the manufacture of plasticware and mattresses in Tanzania and Malawi before moving to Zambia and founding the Lamise company.

The company began operations in Zambia by making pipes for the mines and for irrigation, before expanding into the production of tanks, woven bags and aluminium products (kitchens, windows and doors).

Current activities and products. Lamasat International Zambia makes pipes for the mining and agricultural sectors, plastic water tanks and polypropylene woven bags, as well as office furniture and aluminium products.

It also has a construction division.

Organization and management. The company is run by two brothers who are responsible for the day-to-day management of the business.

Firm capabilities. The company has factories, warehouses and offices in Lusaka and manufactures to meet South African Bureau of Standards quality requirements.

It has the capacity to make 200,000 bags per day.

Supply and marketing chain. The firm imports raw materials for its plastics business from South Korea, South Africa and Turkey; it buys aluminium parts from Lebanon for assembly in Zambia.

Exports. Most products are sold locally, while around 30% are exported to the Democratic Republic of the Congo and Zimbabwe.

15.2.2 Capellaro Investments Ltd

Basic details. Capellaro Investments operates the former parastatal business of Kabwe Industrial Fabrics Limited (KIFCO); it makes polypropylene and polyethylene bags, plastic sheets and twine.

Its annual turnover is approximately US$5 million. The company has around 150 employees.

History. KIFCO was established by the government in 1967 to make jute grain sacks; it later diversified into making woven polypropylene bags, then polyethylene plastic bags, plastic sheeting, refuse bags and polytwine.

The company was privatized in 1996 and was bought by a consortium led by one of its largest customers—Zimbabwe Sugar Refinery (ZSR) (a subsidiary of Tate & Lyle), which acquired 95% of the company's shares—and Knightsbridge Limited, a Zambian company that bought the remaining 5%. As part of the privatization agreement, in 1998 the company installed a US$2.5 million polypropylene plant that was wholly funded by ZSR, resulting in ZSR increasing its shareholding to 97.5%. The jute business was sold in 1998 and a farm was launched to grow kenaf as an alternative source of raw material. The farm was, however, unsuccessful.

In 2001 Tate & Lyle sold ZSR under a management buyout as part of a global strategic repositioning programme, and in 2003 ZSR sold the assets and liabilities of KIFCO to a newly incorporated company, Capellaro Investments, set up by two Zambian companies: Gevano Investments Ltd and Workington Investments Ltd. The Kabwe Industrial Fabrics Limited name was retained by ZSR, while Capellaro Investments registered KIFCO Packaging as a tradename.

In 2009 Technet Zambia Limited acquired 95% of Capellaro Investments from Gevano and Workington Investments, with 5% remaining with Workington. The new owner has recapitalized the company and embarked on a process of refurbishing and replacing machinery.

Current activities and products. Capellaro Investments has two types of product: (branded and unbranded) woven and plastic bags, and polytwine, made from polypropylene. These product lines account for 85% of turnover: the remaining 15% of turnover is generated from the sale of bags and sheets made from polyethylene.

Organization and management. The senior management team comprises the CEO, the chief operating office, the chief accountant and managers for production and quality assurance, sales and marketing, engineering and information technology, and human resources. The CEO reports to a board of directors composed of five members: the two owners, two other family members, and a member with a legal background.

Firm capabilities. The firm is currently operating at full capacity but is limited by the poor state of its equipment, which is the subject of an ongoing rehabilitation strategy.

The company currently produces around 34,000 polypropylene bags per day, compared with 18,000 before the start of the machinery rehabilitation. Planned new equipment is expected to increase capacity to 90,000 bags per day.

Supply and marketing chain. Plastic granules are sourced from South Africa. Since 2012 the company has purchased directly from the main supplier, Sasol, rather than through a South African agent. Middle and Far Eastern sources are cheaper but require larger volume orders than Capellaro Investments can make.

Black plastic sheets and refuse bags are byproducts from recycling waste from the manufacture of clear polyethylene bags, while polytwine is made from recycled waste polypropylene.

A new printer and baler was recently imported from Austria, and larger processing machinery purchases are planned from India.

Most production is sold locally through retailers and distributors, and direct from the Kabwe factory and sales offices in Lusaka and Ndola.

Unreliable supply has been a problem, and the company has lost a number of large agribusiness customers. It is now working to win back key orders.

Exports. Only around 1% of the firm's production is exported—to the Democratic Republic of the Congo, Mozambique and Zimbabwe, or through foreign traders who come to Zambia to buy.

Recent developments. Capellaro Investments has engaged a team of management consultants to help with a rehabilitation plan, including fundraising and the replacement and refurbishment of equipment.

A new extruder was expected to increase output to 1.6 million bags per month.

Development agenda. New equipment is on order that will triple the capacity for making polypropylene bags. There are also plans to introduce laminated products.

15.2.3 Lamise Investments Limited

Basic details. Lamise has 400 employees.

History. Lamise began in the early 1990s when a family of Lebanese origin bought plastics machinery from an existing company.

Current activities and products. Lamise makes household items. Beginning with a product list of around ten items in the early 1990s, it now makes 250 plastic items including basins, chairs, tables and jerrycans, as well as foam mattresses, pillows and sheets.

Organization and management. The company is controlled and run by members of the owning family.

Supply and marketing chain. Raw material inputs are sourced mainly from South Africa (plastic, mould forms), with foam coming from France.

The firm's most risky investments are in new moulds. The company purchased 50 moulds (each costing between US$30,000 and US$50,000) two years ago but 15–20 of these turned out to be unsuccessful because there was no market demand for the products produced from them.

The firm sells through agents in Lusaka, Chipata, Ndola and Kitwe.

Exports. Most products are sold domestically. In the past, the company exported to Zimbabwe, Malawi and Tanzania, but these exports have now stopped due to currency instability.

Chapter 16

MINERALS PROCESSING

16.1 Sector Profile

Background and overview. Zambia is the largest copper producer in Africa and the seventh largest in the world. It is also the world's second largest producer of cobalt, producing 19.7% of total global supply.[1]

Until March 2000 Zambia's mining industry was dominated by Zambia Consolidated Copper Mines (ZCCM), which was formed in 1982. ZCCM was 60.3% owned by the Zambian government, 27.3% owned by Anglo American Plc, and the balance was held by private investors. The liberalization of the economy saw a boost in investment and expansion of mineral production, and ZCCM's assets were sold to the private sector. One of the buyers was Konkola Copper Mines—one of the largest mining and metal companies in the country—which is majority owned (79.4%) by Vedanta Resources. Glencore International and First Quantum Minerals (FQM) acquired the Mufulifa and Nkana divisions of ZCCM—owning 73.1% and 16.9%, respectively, through Mopani Copper Mines. The remaining ZCCM operations have been handed over to ZCCM's successor, ZCCM Investment Holdings, which is 87.6% government owned. Existing and prospective licences and new applications for mining encompass about 50% of Zambia's total landmass.[2]

Recent policies with the intention of diversifying the economy away from its dependence on copper have resulted in exploration for and development of other minerals including cobalt, zinc, manganese and uranium. Government figures put total copper output at a projected 1 million mt per annum in 2012, although figures in the industry expect output to be lower.

[1] *Source*: the website of the Ministry of Mines and Mineral Development at www.zambiamining.co.zm/mininginzambia.htm.

[2] Directory Publishers of Zambia Ltd. 2011/12 *Zambia Review*, 12th edn.

To add value to the ore, copper, lead and zinc ores are smelted before being exported, mostly in cathode form.[3]

Only 5% of Zambian copper is fabricated into end products.[4] Bullion and other metals are recovered from slurries and cobalt is recovered through a leaching process.

Gemstones—mainly emeralds and amethyst—are also an important export for Zambia, with 3.9 million carats produced in the quarter to 31 December 2011.[5]

Profiles and lines of business of large firms. The majority of copper extraction takes place in the Copperbelt, with some prospecting operations in Central, Western and North-Western provinces. The production of copper concentrate is mostly dominated by Konkola Copper Mines Plc, FQM and Mopani Copper Mine. Chambishi Copper Smelter Ltd is a copper processor but it does not mine.

Konkola Copper Mines is 79.4% owned by Vedanta Resources Plc, a London-based metals and mining group. Konkola Copper Mines produced 200,000 mt of copper in total in 2011/12. Output is expected to rise to 400,000 mt on completion of the company's new Konkola Deep Mining Project.

First Quantum Minerals owns 80% of the Kansanshi open-pit copper and gold mine in Solwezi, which produces 250,000 mt of copper per annum, with expansions underway to ramp this up to 400,000 mt per annum by 2015. The company's Trident project is expected to increase overall output through the development of its Sentinel copper deposits located west of Solwezi in the North-Western Province of Zambia.

Mopani Copper Mine, owned by Glencore International and FQM, acquired the Mufulifa and Nkana divisions of ZCCM in 2000 to become Zambia's second largest mine by capacity; it currently produces 113,000 mt of finished copper per annum. An expansion is underway to increase the production of concentrate.

[3] The first stage in copper production is to extract copper from its ore. To do this, the ore is crushed to create a concentrate. Depending on the type of ore—oxide or sulphide—the concentrate is treated through an electrowinning and leaching process or a smelting and electrolytic refining process to remove impurities. It is then processed into a purer solid cathode or blister form, depending on the treatment process, for export. The copper cathode or blister is later used to produce high-purity refined copper. High (A) grade copper cathode is 99.999% copper and is usually made into sheets.

[4] UKAid/World Bank. 2011. What is the potential for more copper fabrication in Zambia? In *Jobs and Prosperity: Building Zambia's Competitiveness Program*.

[5] Directory Publishers of Zambia Ltd. 2011/12. *Zambia Review*, 12th edn.

China Nonferrous Metal Mining (Group) Co., Ltd (CNMC) owns 60% of Copper Smelter Ltd, a Zambian-owned copper processing company with a planned output of 150,000 mt of blister copper ingot and 300,000 mt of sulphuric acid as a byproduct by 2012.

Barrick Gold Corporation bought the Lumwana open-pit mine in North-Western Province, one of the world's largest copper mines, from Equinox Minerals Ltd in 2011. Production only started in 2008 and it has yet to reach full capacity. In 2010 the mine exceeded annual production targets, with an output of 146,000 mt of copper concentrate.

Profiles and lines of business of medium-sized firms. There are a number of medium-sized mining projects underway, including Muliashi Copper Mine, which is expected to start in 2013 with an output of 60,000 mt of copper per annum, and Chambishi Mine, which opened in 2003 and produced 24,000 mt of copper in 2011.

Grizzly Mining mines emeralds and washes them locally for sale to the US, Europe, the Middle East and Asia, employing 411 workers.

Kariba Amethyst Mine, which is 50% owned by London-listed Gemfields Resources, sells to China and India.[6]

Kagem Mining, Zambia's largest emerald producer, is 75% owned by Gemfields, with the government holding 25%. Zambia produces 20% of the world's supply of emeralds.[7]

Small-scale, informal and peripheral activities. The manufacture of copper cables is small compared with copper exports but it is still an important industry. Some foundries produce mill balls from scrap iron, but the serious manufacturers are medium-scale enterprises.

Supply and marketing chain. The price of copper is set by international commodity exchanges,and it is either sold to the metal exchange or directly to traders and end buyers, most of whom are in the Middle East or China.

Export status and potential. Almost all of Zambia's copper is exported, with only 5% remaining in Zambia for fabrication. Research is constantly being undertaken by the mines to extend the life of current mining projects and to find new ways of extracting ore to maximize copper output. The majority of Zambia's copper is exported as cathode or copper blister for use in the manufacture of copper rods and tubes. Copper cathodes are also used for making alloys (with brass, bronze and steel).

[6] Directory Publishers of Zambia Ltd. 2012/13. *Zambia Review*, 13th edn.
[7] Directory Publishers of Zambia Ltd (2012/13).

Policy context. The government has adopted policies designed to enhance investment in the mining industry. The right to explore for or produce minerals is authorized by a licence granted under the Mines and Minerals Act, and mining policy is enacted through three departments: Geological Survey, Mines Development and Mines Safety. Some key objectives of mining policy include diversifying mineral-based products and exports, encouraging the small-scale mining industry, ensuring that investors secure titles to mining rights, and providing a stable fiscal regime and allowing foreign exchange retention.

Industry executives claim that the fiscal regime is unstable, with development agreements arbitrarily set aside in 2008 with major tax increases, a doubling of Mineral Royalty Tax in 2012, and a reduction in the capital allowances available in the 2013 budget.

The government does not directly participate in exploration or other mining activities and has a predominantly regulatory and promotional role. There is, however, some dispute within the mining industry about how total copper output is reported and recorded. The mining industry reckons that government exaggerates copper output, with one key area of confusion being the duplicated recording of copper output during processing of third-party copper concentrate. In addition, there are concerns that the sector's contribution to foreign exchange earnings and GDP is underestimated.

Taxation levels for the industry are hotly debated, with some advocating a windfall tax on the sector. Industry executives complain of comparatively high tax rates and uncertainty in policies.

16.2 Profiles of Major Firms

16.2.1 First Quantum Minerals Ltd (FQM)

Basic details. FQM, a Canadian company, operates the Kansanshi open-pit copper and gold mine, one of the largest copper mines in Africa, providing the company with three-quarters of its turnover.

The mine has 1,515 direct employees, and total employment including employment via contractors is 9,500. It is one of the country's largest employers.

Globally, FQM recorded turnover of US$2.58 billion in 2011, of which US$1.9 billion was derived from the Kansanshi mine. All the copper mined was exported as concentrate or cathode.

The company is listed on the Toronto and London stock exchanges.

History. FQM was incorporated in 1983. It acquired Zambia's oldest mine, Bwana Mkubwa, in 1996. This mine has now ceased copper production as reserves are depleted but it is still a source of sulphuric acid. The company currently operates three mines, with four further projects under development worldwide. In 1998 it completed construction of the Bwana Mkubwa copper cathode solvent extraction and electrowinning tailings retreatment and sulphuric acid plant; in 2000 it acquired an interest in Mopani Copper Mines in Zambia with Glencore.

FQM owns 16.9% of Carlisa Ltd, which in turn owns 90% of Mopani Copper Mines, with ZCCM holding the remaining 10%. The main assets of Mopani Copper Mines are its Mufulira division—the former assets of ZCCM—and the Nkana mine concentrator and cobalt plant. In 2001 FQM acquired an 80% interest in the Kansanshi open-pit copper and gold mine near Solwezi. Commercial production began in 2005.

The company also has operations in Mauritania and Western Australia.

Current activities and products. The company currently produces LME grade A copper cathode, copper concentrate, nickel, gold and sulphuric acid. At Kansanshi, flexible ore treatment allows for variation in ore type: there is a sulphide circuit, an oxide circuit and a gold facility. Approximately half of its production is in the form of finished copper cathode. FQM also has two other projects underway in Zambia: Sentinel and Enterprise.

Organization and management. A nine-member board of directors comprising the chairman and CEO, two other executive directors and six independent directors oversees the company's operations.

Firm capabilities. Kansanshi mine is the biggest copper producer in Africa, with output of 240,000 mt per annum at full capacity. By the end of 2014 annual output is expected to reach 400,000 mt, most of which will be processed at the company's own smelter.

Supply and marketing chain. Capital goods, from crushers to mills and mining equipment, are sourced from manufacturers in the US, Europe and Sweden, with a small proportion coming from South Africa.

Exports. From a low of US$2,812 per mt in December 2008, the average price of copper on the international market rose to US$7,202 per mt between January and September 2010. Furthermore, with the resumption of production at a number of copper mines and new investments boosting production levels at others, copper output rose by 17.7% in 2010, reaching a record high of 820,000 mt. Copper is traded on the LME and sold to metal traders internationally. Metal traders supply to end users, mostly in China and the Far East. FQM holds about one-third of the country's market share and the majority of its copper is exported in cathode form.

Recent developments. Construction has just started on the company's Sentinel project, which is part of a wider project located approximately 150 km west of Kansanshi mine. Plans are underway to develop Sentinel into a state-of-the-art facility capable of producing up to 300,000 mt of copper concentrate annually.

The company's strategy is to develop this facility over a two-year period, during which it will build a new copper smelter in Zambia that will process all of Sentinel's concentrate production. These twin smelter projects will require a capital investment of more than US$2.4 billion, including an extensive infrastructure development programme, and create approximately 2,400 direct local jobs.

Globally, the company expects to triple its annual copper production capacity, positioning it within the world's ten largest copper producers. In 2011 production reached 265,576 mt of copper and 175,225 ounces of gold across all projects.

16.2.2 Konkola Copper Mines Plc (KCM)

Basic details. KCM mines and refines copper. Its turnover was US$1.7 billion for the financial year ending in March 2012. The company has 22,000 employees, 8,000 of whom are in full-time employment; it is the largest private-sector employer in Zambia.

History. KCM was set up in 1982 and was owned by the Anglo American Corporation and Roan Selection Trust. The mines were then nationalized in the 1970s and taken over by the formerly government-owned ZCCM, before finally being unbundled during privatization. Anglo American acquired a 51% stake in KCM in September 2002 but sold its shares to Vedanta Resources in 2004. In 2008 Vedanta Resources, a global metals and mining group, increased its holding in the company to 79.4%. The remaining 20.6% interest is held by ZCCM Investment Holdings, which is 87.6% owned by the Zambian government.

Current activities and products. KCM is a major integrated copper producer in Zambia, with an underground copper mine at Konkola, underground and open-pit copper and cobalt mines at Nchanga, and a pyrite mine at Nampundwe.

KCM has several processing plants: the new Konkola concentrator processes ore sourced from the Konkola underground mine to produce a copper flotation concentrate for subsequent smelting. At Nchanga, the company recently commissioned two new concentrators that are used to produce both copper and cobalt concentrates.

The Nchanga smelter converts copper concentrates into copper anodes and a copper–cobalt alloy, while the Nchanga acid plant produces sulphuric acid used in the treatment and extraction of copper at the tailings leach plant.

The Nchanga tailings leach plant is used for the production of copper cathodes from processing the tailings from the Nchanga concentrates.

The Nkana refinery processes the anodes from the Changa smelter into LME grade copper cathodes that are sold to domestic and international customers.

KCM produces two types of copper cathode: the Nkana refinery produces grade A copper cathode, which is listed on the LME.

The company also treats concentrates purchased from other mines at its Nchanga smelter and Nkana refinery. Total output of copper cathode for the financial year that ended in March 2012 was 200,000 mt.

Organization and management. KCM's CEO is seconded by Vedanta. The company has two executive directors for Nchanga and Konkola. The management team includes a chief financial officer, a director of strategy and business development, and a technical director.

Firm capabilities. Since its original acquisition, Vedanta has invested more than US$2.5 billion in upgrading equipment, building new facilities and expanding capacity. Operations at the Nchanga smelter are currently increasing towards full capacity and the smelter has already achieved rated capability in capacity and recovery. The Nchanga smelter is designed to process copper concentrate mined at KCM's mines, but it can also process third-party copper concentrate mixed with KCM's concentrate. The smelter's operating output therefore depends on the amount of copper concentrate produced by KCM's mines and on demand from third parties to process concentrate. This smelter is also one of the most environmentally friendly smelters in the world, with benchmark sulphur capture of greater than 99%.

Supply and marketing chain. Machinery is imported from South Africa and Europe; chemicals used in recovering concentrates, and consumables such as oil, lime and heavy fuel oil, are sourced locally. KCM's main acid plant at Nchanga produces sulphuric acid from off-gases produced by the Nchanga smelter. Captured sulphur dioxide gas is recycled into sulphuric acid, which is then utilized in the tailings leach operations or sold. Anode slimes from the company's refining operations at Nkana are sold on long-term contracts. Copper–cobalt alloy is marketed to cobalt processing plants. Excess sulphuric acid is exported to the Democratic Republic of the Congo or sold locally to Chambishi Metals and Kansanshi Mines.

Copper cathodes are supplied to ZAMEFA.

Exports. Copper cathode is sold directly to long-term customers in China and the Middle East, and to local traders. It is exported by rail or truck. Rail transportation is preferred given the high cost of road freight at a capacity of only 30 mt per truck.

Recent developments. The Konkola Deep Mining Project will expand the production of copper ore from 2 million mt to 7.5 million mt per annum. The cost of the project is nearly US$1 billion. Further exploration techniques are under consideration with a view to increasing the ratio of copper extracted from the ore and to expanding the life of current mining operations.

16.2.3 Scaw Limited

Basic details. Scaw's core business is the manufacture of grinding media balls and castings. Turnover was US$10 million for the year that ended in March 2012, including exports at US$2 million. The company employs 500 full-time staff and a small number of casual staff not engaged on the production line.

History. Scaw Limited was formally incorporated in 1960 when the Tow brothers went into partnership with Scaw Metals Limited of South Africa to manufacture grinding balls and metals and the name was changed to Scaw-Tow Foundries Limited. The Tow brothers were later bought out and the company's name was changed to Scaw Limited in May 1974. In January 1989 the nationalized ZCCM acquired the major shareholding in Scaw Limited from Scaw Metals Limited; it was subsequently run as a subsidiary of Zal Holdings (a subsidiary of ZCCM) until 1992, at which point it became a direct subsidiary of ZCCM. In 1998 the firm was sold to Beekay Engineering and Castings Limited of India. The shareholding of the company was reorganized and restructured in order to raise financial resources for recapitalization, modernization and diversification, and it was then sold to a holding company based in Mauritius.

Current activities and products. The company's main products are

- grinding media balls, both low-chrome and high-chrome;
- hammer-forged grinding media balls suitable for semi-autogenous grinding (SAG) mills;
- steel, iron, manganese, heat-resistant and high-alloy castings;
- deformed bars; and
- industrial gases.

The company has an installed capacity of 36,000 mt of the above products per annum. Total production of all products is projected at 20,000 mt for 2013. The company has recently set up a forging plant to manufacture hammer-forged grinding media balls for SAG mills operated by the mines. The company has also developed a number of new cast items for the mines to substitute for imports. Other items that the company manufactures include mill liners, ball liners, crusher liners, jaw plates, lifter bars, trunnion liners, metal liners, hammers, pipes, pencil ingots, heat-resistant castings and high-chrome liners. SAG mill liners are now being developed and Scaw holds more than 20,000 patents for the manufacture of various additional castings for ingots and deformed bars that are not mentioned in the above list.

Organization and management. Mr R. D. Gupta is the company CEO. He is supported by a technical director, a finance director and a marketing director.

Firm capabilities. The firm's total capacity is 36,000 mt per annum. Progress in the mining sector has boosted business, which has risen in the last two years, and the plant is expected to operate at roughly 60–70% of capacity in 2012.

Competition. There are more than a dozen, mostly Chinese, companies making low-chrome grinding media balls locally but no one else is yet producing high-chrome balls, forged balls or castings.

Supply and marketing chain. The company imports around 40% of inputs: refractories, ramming mass, ferroalloys, quenching oil, electrical and hardware items, engineering equipment and spare parts. The major local input is steel scrap, which is collected from mines, farms, workshops, scrap dealers and contractors.

Most sales of mill balls and castings are made to the mines (Konkola Copper Mines, Mopani and FQM). The company's products are customized and relationships with end users are important.

Scaw also sells deformed bars and other construction materials to between 600 and 700 local customers, with contracts established through direct marketing.

Policy context. Competition in producing high-chrome balls, forged balls and castings is mainly from imported stock from South Africa and elsewhere in the SADC and COMESA regions. These imports are almost duty free, while Scaw and other local manufacturers pay duty on the import of the consumable items used in the production process. Another factor affecting local manufacturers is the economies of scale at which SADC and COMESA manufacturers are operating. For example, South Africa is producing over 1,000,000 mt of balls annually whereas Scaw's annual production is 20,000 mt. If imports of manufactured goods were restricted for a period, especially from SADC and COMESA countries, then local industry believes it would have an opportunity to grow. Presently, Scaw has a low market share (about 30%) due to imports.

Exports. Roughly 10–15% of the company's output is exported to the Democratic Republic of the Congo and to mines in Botswana.

Recent developments. Scaw is currently installing a second forging hammer and associated equipment. Once both hammers are operational, Scaw will employ an additional 60–80 workers. To expand production of high-chrome balls, Scaw is planning to set up a semi-automatic production line with a capacity of 24,000 mt per annum of high-chrome grinding media balls and 10,000 mt per annum of SAG mill liners. At an estimated cost of about US$50 million, this will create 300 additional direct jobs and 200 additional indirect jobs. Scaw also plans to set up an additional 50,000 mt per annum plant for manufacturing forged balls at a total estimated cost of US$30 million; this will create 1,000 additional direct jobs, provided that the company's efforts are supported by the mines and the government.

16.2.4 Chambishi Copper Smelter Limited

Basic details. Chambishi Copper Smelter, a copper processing company, employs 1,200 permanent workers and had a turnover of US$1.35 billion in 2011.

History. The firm was registered in Zambia in July 2006 with a total investment of US$300 million. It is 60% owned by CNMC and 40% owned by Yunnan Copper Industry Group Company Limited.

Current activities and products. The firm produces copper blisters, sulphuric acid, copper ingots and bagged cobalt–copper alloys.

Organization and management. Chambishi Copper Smelter is run by five directors supported by professional departments heads (covering the technical, business development, human resources and accounts departments).

Firm capabilities. It has ISA technology for the production of copper and sulphuric acid. A top submerged oxygen enrichment smelting process is used, with an electric smelting furnace and a Peirce–Smith converter blowing process.

Supply and marketing chain. The company sources all its materials locally. It produces 150,000 mt of blister copper per annum and 300,000 mt of sulphuric acid.

Exports. Its products are exported to international markets including the US. The company exports some 50% of its sulphuric acid and all of its blister copper.

Development agenda. The firm intends to expand its copper smelting, while developing comprehensive recycling.